D1401996

Ask a
Franciscan

ANSWERS TO
CATHOLIC
QUESTIONS

PAT McCLOSKEY, O.F.M.

ST. ANTHONY MESSENGER PRESS
Cincinnati, Ohio

Nihil Obstat: Hilarion Kistner, O.F.M.
Imprimi Potest: Fred Link, O.F.M.

RESCRIPT

In accord with the *Code of Canon Law*, I hereby grant the *Imprimatur* ("Permission to Publish") to *Ask a Franciscan: Answers to Catholic Questions* by Pat McCloskey, O.F.M.

Reverend Joseph R. Binzer
Vicar General
Archdiocese of Cincinnati
Cincinnati, Ohio
August 20, 2010

The *Imprimatur* ("Permission to Publish") is a declaration that a book or pamphlet is considered to be free from doctrinal or moral error. It is not implied that those who have granted the *Imprimatur* agree with the contents, opinions or statements expressed.

Scripture passages have been taken from *New Revised Standard Version Bible*, copyright ©1989 by the Division of Christian Education of the National Council of the Churches of Christ in the U.S.A., and used by permission. All rights reserved.

Cover and book design by Mark Sullivan
Cover image © Irochka | Dreamstime.com

LIBRARY OF CONGRESS CATALOGING-IN-PUBLICATION DATA
McCloskey, Patrick.
Ask a Franciscan : answers to Catholic questions / Pat McCloskey.
p. cm.
ISBN 978-0-86716-970-6 (alk. paper)
1. Catholic Church—Doctrines—Miscellanea. I. Title.
BX1754.3.M33 2010
230'.2—dc22
2010025602

ISBN 978-0-86716-970-6

Published by St. Anthony Messenger Press
28 W. Liberty St.
Cincinnati, OH 45202
www.AmericanCatholic.org
www.SAMPBooks.org

Printed in the United States of America.

Printed on acid-free paper.

10 11 12 13 14   5 4 3 2 1

CONTENTS

Introduction

Each person brings a unique personal history to his or her growth in faith. Even though we speak of a childhood faith, a teen faith, a young adult faith, a middle-aged faith, and a senior faith, every person within the same age group has not faced identical challenges to faith. Someone at age thirty-seven may experience a crisis that another person faced at age nineteen. Every crisis is both a danger and an opportunity.

Although adults do not expect to wear the same shoes as they did at age five, we are sometimes tempted to think that our faith has already grown enough. Some people find it difficult to link *faith* and *growth*.

God, the object of our faith, does not need to grow. But, like all relationships, our relationship with God will either grow or wither. Just as the opposite of love is not hate but indifference, so the opposite of a living faith is not atheism but a "good enough" faith that resists further growth.

The man whose son was cured of evils spirits called out to Jesus, "I believe; help my unbelief!" (Mark 9:24). On the road to Emmaus, Jesus explained to two disciples several Scripture passages that they thought they already understood. "Were not our hearts burning within us while he was talking to us on the road, while he was opening the scriptures to us?" they asked (Luke 24:32). In the Scriptures and in the Eucharist, they recognized him and grew in their faith.

This book collects ninety-seven questions and my answers from the almost six hundred that have appeared in St. *Anthony Messenger* between September 1999 and January 2010 in our "Ask the Wise Man" or "Ask a Franciscan" column. Some responses have been revised.

Many entries cite *St. Anthony Messenger* articles, editorials, or columns that can be found in the magazine's electronic archive at www.AmericanCatholic.org, which is the website of St. Anthony Messenger Press. Several entries in this book refer to issues of *Catholic Update*, an adult education newsletter that began in 1973. It, too, has an electronic archive at the company site and many of its issues since April 1996 can be read there. A resources page gives the web addresses and toll-free numbers cited in this book.

In writing this column, I have accumulated too many debts to acknowledge completely here. John Feister and Hilarion Kistner, O.F.M., have reviewed each column and pointed out things to be added, clarified, or deleted. Proofreaders have prevented many mistakes. Because of their knowledge, I have called upon Thomas Richstatter, O.F.M. (liturgy), Donald Miller, O.F.M., and Daniel Kroger, O.F.M. (moral theology), and Hilarion Kistner, O.F.M. (Scripture), and other experts. I thank Kathleen Carroll, who edited this book.

Norman Perry, O.F.M., my predecessor in writing this column under various titles for thirty-three years, conveyed both knowledge and pastoral sensitivity that I have striven to continue.

May all of us continue to grow as disciples of Jesus!

CHAPTER ONE

How We Understand God

Can God Hate Anyone?

In Romans 9:13, Saint Paul reflects on God's free choice of people. Paul presents God as saying, "I have loved Jacob, / but I have hated Esau" (quoting Malachi 1:2–3). Can God really hate?

The *New American Bible's* footnote for Romans 9:13 reads: "The literal rendering 'Jacob I loved, but Esau I hated,' suggests an attitude of divine hostility that is not implied in Paul's statement. In Semitic usage *hate* means to love less; see Luke 14:26, with Matthew 10:37. Israel's unbelief reflects the mystery of the divine election that is always operative within it. Mere natural descent from Abraham does not ensure the full possession of the divine gifts; it is God's sovereign prerogative to bestow this fullness upon, or to withhold it from, whomsoever he wishes; see Matthew 3:9 and John 8:39. The choice of Jacob over Esau is a case in point."

Jacob was Esau's twin (but younger) brother. God chooses people for God's own reasons.

Why Does God Sometimes Seem Aloof and Impersonal?

During a recent trip, I listened to a course entitled "Faith and Reason: Philosophy in the Middle Ages." I must say that I found Anselm's proof for God's existence to be more clever than persuasive. Similarly, the proofs of Saint Thomas Aquinas are not exactly airtight. How do Franciscan scholars feel about proofs of God's existence? I think that Søren Kierkegaard had it right when he spoke of a "leap of faith." I think God is beyond our ability to grasp—other than a few blessed snippets—much less prove. Thus belief or not is a choice we make.

"Proofs" for God's existence rely exclusively on the evidence of reason. Proofs from order, causality, Anselm's ontological proof and others are in this category. This is fine as far as it goes. Saint Anselm (d.1109) famously described theology as "faith seeking understanding." He employed reason to draw out the implications of his faith.

Reason alone tends to "prove" an impersonal God—a pale imitation of the loving, generous God revealed in the Scriptures. The pagan philosopher Aristotle spoke of the "Unmoved Mover." This is logical but cold. Reason may prove a Supreme Being but hardly a God who creates people in the divine image and wants to share divine life with them.

Deism, a system of thought favored by the eighteenth-century Enlightenment but still alive today, favors an aloof, minimalist God who sets the world in motion and then moves on to something else. Deism is ultimately not comfortable with God's self-revelation in the Bible. For example, Thomas Jefferson produced an edited version of the New Testament, emphasizing Jesus as a moral teacher but deleting all references to Christ's divinity or to his miracles.

In modern terminology, that might be called a "good-enough Jesus." Deism favors a "good-enough God," but one who falls far short of the God revealed in the Scriptures.

I was mulling over this response when Advent began. A ninth-century Latin hymn, sung especially in Advent, is titled *Creator Alme Siderum* (Loving Creator of the Stars). Deists could certainly accept *Creator Siderum*, but only God's self-revelation in the Bible justifies the all-important adjective *Alme* (Loving).

Only a loving God explains the Incarnation of Jesus; only a loving God can be compared to the forgiving father in the Prodigal Son parable. Can a strictly logical proof for God rely much on love? Love, however, is the main reason why anything other than God even exists. You and I can ask questions about proving God's existence only because *we* already exist—made possible through God's love.

Deism implicitly tends toward atheism because people eventually start asking, "Who needs such an impersonal, aloof God?" The Bible doesn't say that God is impersonal or aloof, but reason alone cannot get beyond that hurdle. Faith is not against reason, but it is beyond reason.

Pope John Paul II's 1998 encyclical, Faith and Reason, and many writings of Pope Benedict XVI address these and related issues. From its earliest days, Christianity has spoken of "natural law." That terminology assumes that reason has a role to play in understanding God. This concept made dialogue with pagan philosophers possible.

Franciscan scholars such as Alexander of Hales, Saint Bonaventure, and Blessed John Duns Scotus (all thirteenth-century teachers in Paris) upheld the compatibility of faith and reason. To do otherwise would mean one of two errors: fideism (reason has nothing to contribute to faith) or rationalism (faith cannot contribute anything to reason). Even so, Franciscan thinkers have always emphasized the importance of God's loving will to create, to share life—something that cannot be proven by reason alone.

Enlightenment thinkers saw biblical faith as the enemy of human progress. In fact, such faith is ultimately a very strong ally of genuine progress.

We know that what is done in the name of reason is not always reasonable. Intolerance of various kinds can be made to look reasonable. Faith offers a transcendent viewpoint to help us see the difference between a pseudo-reason to the advantage of some people and the real thing. If someone uses reason to rule out any transcendent dimension to human life, tyranny cannot be far behind. Pope John Paul II's 2005 book, *Memory and Identity: Conversations at the Dawn of a Millennium*, explores these themes.

Both faith and reason are gifts from God.

Was Jesus Jewish?

If Jesus was Jewish, why don't Catholics follow Jewish teachings?

Catholics follow many Jewish teachings, such as the Ten Commandments. Catholic Sunday Masses almost always include a reading from the Hebrew Scriptures and a Psalm response. The Mass prayer "Blessed are you, Lord, God of all creation. Through your goodness we have this bread [wine] to offer..." comes from Judaism.

When a second-century Christian said that the God of the Hebrew Scriptures was not the same as the God of the New Testament, the Catholic Church described such teaching as heresy. Jesus was born Jewish and cannot be understood apart from Judaism.

Jesus also preached about a kingdom of God which is open to Jews and non-Jews (gentiles). The Letter to the Ephesians says that Christ broke down the wall between Jews and gentiles, reconciling both with God (2:11–17).

Some Jewish people accepted that teaching while others did not. Those who did so became Christians, willing to call Jesus the Son of God. Not surprisingly, other Jews felt such a title undermined the absolute bedrock of Judaism, their belief in one God.

For the first forty years after Jesus' death, many people regarded Christianity as a group within Judaism. As the Good News spread, so many gentiles were baptized that eventually they became the majority within Christianity.

Why Was Jesus Baptized?

I don't understand why Jesus was baptized by Saint John the Baptist. Everyone else whom John baptized had sinned and was showing sorrow by means of receiving baptism. That was not the case with Jesus. Also, Christian baptism wipes away original sin, but Christ did not have that.

Jesus had not committed any sin and thus did not need to be baptized. According to Matthew 3:14, John initially declined, saying that he needed to be baptized by Jesus. Our Lord responded, "Let it be so for now, for it is proper for us in this way to fulfill all righteousness."

The baptism of Jesus is part of his self-revelation and the formal start of his ministry. In its liturgy, the church links the birth of Jesus, his manifestation to the Magi and his baptism years later.

Several Old Testament prophets had visions that inaugurated their ministry (see Isaiah 6:1–13, for example). The baptism of Jesus is the first indication in the Gospels of the Trinity, with the voice of God the Father and the dove representing the Holy Spirit (see also Mark 1:10–11 and Luke 3:21–22).

If baptism is the sacrament through which people enter the church, it seems fitting that Jesus shows the way—identifying with sinners though he was sinless.

Did Jesus Despair?

One of the Gospels presents Jesus as saying on the cross, "My God, my God, why have you forsaken me?" Was Jesus despairing of God's love and care?

If your Bible gives cross references, it should tell you that this verse from Matthew 27:46 is actually a quote from Psalm 22:2. Matthew 27:35 and 27:43 are also based on verses from Psalm 22, the prayer of an innocent person.

Matthew expected that his Jewish-Christian audience (Christians who were born Jewish) would recognize these references from the Hebrew Scriptures. His Gospel uses many such references to show the continuity between Jesus and the Old Testament. Luke 24:46 presents Jesus as quoting Psalm 31 ("Into your hands, I commend my spirit....) just before he died. Jesus did not despair.

Are Catholics Concerned About the Wrong Things?

It seems that lately Catholics are more concerned with keeping traditions, how sacraments are to be performed, than with learning how to have a more intimate relationship with the Lord. Does God really care how many candles we light in front of a statue or when the Gloria is sung?

Why do we pray to saints? They don't answer prayers; God does. Since when did God stop having time to listen and answer our prayers? Isn't there more to our faith than lighting candles and other traditions? When people ask me why I am a Catholic, I want to be able to say more than "I was born a Catholic."

The sacraments are community prayer, reflecting and deepening one's personal relationship with the Lord. In order for people to join in public prayer, its celebration needs a recognizable shape. Although it can help prayer, ritual is not an end in itself. Lighting a candle is a sacramental, an action or object that reminds people of God's presence and mercy.

Yes, some Catholics go through the motions without a deepening conversion. But other people can do that while claiming to seek a more intimate relationship with the Lord. Perhaps that was the problem that prompted Jesus to say, "Not everyone who says to me, 'Lord, Lord,' will enter the kingdom of heaven, but only the one who does the will of my Father in heaven" (Matthew 7:21).

Catholicism is a sacramental religion, which believes that God can act even through the public prayers of its members—some of whom can be overly fussy about its details.

Saints are not an alternative to God but instead remind us that cooperating with God's grace (holiness) can take many forms. Jesus never dealt with a delinquent son as Saint Monica did. God never faced political pressure (renounce God or die) as martyrs did. Catholicism worships God but venerates saints, who always point us back to God.

Since the beginning, Jesus' followers have been pondering and praying over the Scriptures as Mary did (Luke 2:19 and 2:51). Aren't words like *faith* and *journey* a big part of why you remain Catholic?

How Are We Saved?

Ephesians 2:8 says, "For by grace you have been saved through faith, and this is not your own doing; it is the gift of God—." Jesus alone is the sacrifice for our sins. We can do nothing of our own merit except to believe and have faith in our Risen Lord, Jesus Christ.

Indulgences should not, therefore, be needed if a person has faith in Jesus Christ and his saving gift of salvation. Indulgences suggest that Jesus' death on the cross was useless.

Some people speak of faith as though it were exclusively an activity of the mind. Your "believe-and-have-faith" statement sounds close to that understanding of faith. Other people believe—and the Catholic Church teaches—that genuine faith already includes a person's response to God's grace. In Galatians 5:6, Saint Paul says, "For in Christ Jesus, neither circumcision nor uncircumcision counts for anything, the only thing that counts is faith *working through love* [emphasis added]."

The Catholic Church understands an indulgence to be the full or partial remission of temporal punishment for a sin that has already been confessed and forgiven. No one needs indulgences in order to be saved. But everyone who is saved does need a faith that is more than saying, "Lord, Lord" (Matthew 7:21). Jesus says that a faith-filled person must seek to do God's will.

Indulgences are linked to the concept of "temporal punishment due to sin" because every sin has built-in negative consequences that have a life of their own.

I could tell a lie about you and later repent of it and be forgiven in the sacrament of penance. Would my repentance guarantee that this lie will stop—even if I told the truth to everyone to whom I told that lie? No.

My repentance for a particular sin does not wipe away that sin's ongoing, negative consequences. Jesus' disciples must learn to accept that part of reality.

The temporal punishment due to sin has immediate consequences for the sinner. He or she realizes that sin hurts a person's relationship with God; repentance is part of mending that relationship and of living it out more completely.

Jesus alone saves. If I think, however, that saying, "Lord, Lord" is enough, I am mistaken. I need to acknowledge that every sin is, in fact, not a shortcut to something good but a dead end. God invites us to use our freedom in a way that is worthy of someone made in God's image and likeness.

Faith always involves a response—not to impress God but to allow God's grace to bear fruit, to affect our decisions radically.

Are There Any Feminine Images of God?

Is there a reference to the Holy Spirit as a "mother eagle" in the book of Isaiah? If so, where?

You may be thinking of Deuteronomy 32:11 which says, "As an eagle stirs up its nest, / and hovers over its young; as it spreads its wings, takes them up, / and bears them aloft on its pinions,…" In fact, the eagle here is a mother eagle.

That verse is part of a longer hymn (32:1–43) in praise of God. Verse 18 says, "You were unmindful of the Rock that bore you; you forgot the God who gave you birth."

The book of Isaiah has at least three references to God using feminine imagery: God's anguish for the Israelites is like that of a woman giving birth (42:14), God cherishes them with a mother's love (49:15) and, "As a mother comforts her son, so will I comfort you" (66:13).

You can find more information about feminine images of God in *Women and the Word: The Gender of God in the New Testament and the Spirituality of Women*, by Sandra Schneiders, I.H.M. (Paulist).

No Old Testament writer understood God the Holy Spirit as Christians now do because the doctrine of the Trinity had not yet been revealed.

CHAPTER TWO

How We Relate to Mary and the Other Saints

Did Mary Have Real Freedom?

A friend of mine believes that Mary did not have free will as other humans do. Therefore, the mother of Jesus had no choice except to say yes to the Archangel Gabriel at the Annunciation. This friend believes that our all-knowing God knew that Mary was going to say yes and thus she was not about to say no after God had created her immaculate in her conception.

Your friend is wrong on one count and right on another. God is indeed all-knowing, but why should God's foreknowledge of what Mary would say be any different from God's foreknowledge of your decisions or my decisions?

Your friend is assuming that God is limited by time the way that we humans are. You are more present to me than Julius Caesar or Florence Nightingale because you are alive and they are not. Human beings can only live sequentially; that is a limitation that God does not share. You, I, Julius Caesar, and Florence Nightingale are all equally present to God. The term *foreknowledge* as applied to God is not very helpful because it presumes that God lives, as we do, sequentially.

If you took your friend's position to an extreme, wouldn't God's fore-knowledge about Adolf Hitler and Mother Teresa of Calcutta make God equally responsible for their vastly different actions? If God is not responsible for their personal decisions, why should God have toyed with Mary's freedom at the Annunciation?

Human freedom is very real and can produce very different results. God's knowledge does not cancel out human freedom—for good or for ill. God freely created everything that exists. Our being made in God's image means that we have a limited but very real freedom, which we need to use wisely and generously.

Mary can inspire us to grow as disciples. The generosity that she showed at the Annunciation can help in that process.

How Much Did Mary Know?

When Mary was invited by the Archangel Gabriel to be the mother of Jesus, did she know any details about Jesus' future life? Where he would be born? What he would do as an adult? That he would be crucified, rise from the dead, and ascend into heaven?

Mary probably knew none of those details beforehand. If she had, Mary might have gone through life with an I-know-but-can't-tell-you smirk on her face. Living with uncertainty flowed from Mary's reply to Gabriel: "Here am I, the servant of the Lord; let it be with me according to your word" (Luke 1:38a). Mary had to take life as it came—just as we do.

Saint Luke tells us a great deal when he writes that after the visit from the shepherds outside Bethlehem, "...Mary treasured all these words and pondered them in her heart" (2:19). After Jesus at age twelve was lost in the Temple for three days and then returned to Nazareth with Mary and Joseph, Saint Luke notes, "His mother treasured all these things in her heart" (2:51b).

In a way, Mary anticipated the two disciples on the road to Emmaus (Luke 24:13–35) by bringing the puzzling events of her life to prayer, by seeking help from Scripture to understand them. This is what makes Mary the first and most perfect disciple of Jesus, as the late Father Raymond Brown, S.S., described so well in a May 1997 magazine article for *St. Anthony Messenger.*

Mary knows our struggles and our joys. Perhaps that is why paintings and statues of Mary holding Jesus after he was taken down from the cross have been very popular across cultures and down through the centuries. This is not the end of her story, but she had to live this part to arrive at the end.

Where would faith have been if Mary had known the details of Jesus' life but had hid them? According to Hebrews 11:1, "Faith is the assurance of things hoped for, the conviction of things not seen."

Henry Alford's hymn text describes Mary's faith as well as ours: "We walk by faith, and not by sight / No gracious words we hear / of him who spoke as none e'er spoke / but we believe him near." Mary did a good deal of soul-searching before she heard Jesus speak—as well as much pondering and praying after Jesus ascended into heaven.

Are Apparitions of Mary Real?

What does the Catholic Church teach about apparitions of Mary? Does the church support these sightings? Some priests support these enthusiastically and others do not. I was taught to respect the mother of Jesus.

Apparitions may be genuine—for example, Tepeyac (Our Lady of Guadalupe), Lourdes, and Fatima. There have also been cases where the church has judged them not to be genuine—for example, Bayside, New York, where Mary is said to have appeared and denounced many of the liturgical changes authorized by Vatican II.

Any apparition must be judged in relation to the Scriptures and Tradition as the church prayerfully interprets these. Not even a genuine apparition can be part of the "deposit of faith" (see 1 Timothy 6:20 and 2 Timothy 1:12, 14). In other words, you could deny that Mary appeared at Lourdes—I am not suggesting or encouraging this!—and you would not be denying your faith on the same level as if you denied Jesus' real presence in the Eucharist.

Great respect should be shown to Mary; she is Jesus' first and most perfect disciple. Some people, however, have used reports of Marian apparitions to legitimate things they could not otherwise credibly promote. People have sometimes hijacked genuine devotion to Mary to promote their own or some group's agenda.

In the final chapter of Vatican II's Dogmatic Constitution on the Church, the bishops reminded Catholics that "true devotion consists neither in sterile or transitory feeling, nor in an empty credulity, but proceeds from true faith, by which we are led to recognize the excellence of the Mother of God, and we are moved to a filial love towards our mother and to the imitation of her virtues" (#67).

In *The Dictionary of Mary*, Anthony Buono writes: "It is true that Church authority has recognized the apparitions at Guadalupe, Lourdes, Knock and Fatima; and John Paul II has visited these four shrines. However, the Church does not oblige her members to believe in such apparitions. In these cases, in fact, the Church says only that there are good reasons to believe, that such places have borne fruit but she never demands belief. Everyone remains free to believe or not."

In his 1987 encyclical *Redemptoris Mater*, The Mother of the Redeemer, Pope John Paul II emphasized Mary's role in guiding Jesus' followers on their pilgrimage of faith (sections 42 through 47). We can best show respect for Mary by imitating her generosity in responding to God's grace.

Do Saints Hear Our Prayers?

Can saints in heaven hear our prayers? According to a former Catholic, people are wasting their time praying to the saints. Does Scripture help on this issue?

Saints in heaven hear us but cannot answer prayers independently of God. We do not pray to saints because they are an alternative to God, for example, the way a child may seek to obtain from one parent something that the other parent has turned down.

We pray to saints because they are outstanding examples of how to cooperate generally with God's grace. Their example helps us do the same. That is the spirit in which chapter eleven of the Letter to the Hebrews praises holy men and women in the Hebrew Scriptures.

In praying for saintly intercession, we are asking that the saints join their prayers to ours. They encourage us to join them at the river of life-giving water that flows from the throne of God (see Revelation 22:1).

Why Are There So Few Lay Saints?

Few laypeople have been formally canonized. Although most saints belonged to religious communities, people in that state of life make up a tiny percentage of the church. Doesn't the present system suggest that only priests and vowed religious can become saints? That's not very inspiring.

The formal canonization process requires a group of people interested in seeing someone beatified and then canonized. Although some dioceses have promoted the cause of laypeople, you are correct that most often it is religious communities who support the process for someone to be declared venerable, have a miracle authenticated, then be formally beatified, have a second miracle authenticated, and eventually be canonized.

At present, most laypeople who are blesseds or saints were either martyrs (Thomas More or Maria Goretti, for example) or single people (Kateri Tekakwitha or Julian of Norwich). On October 21, 2001, Pope John Paul II beatified Luigi Beltrame Quattrocchi and Maria Corsini, the married parents of four children, three of whom entered religious communities. This is a step in the right direction but is a mixed message.

The church identifies blesseds and saints not for their benefit but for the church's sake—to show that holiness is possible in every century, every walk of life, every part of the globe, and in every circumstance of life. If saints already enjoy eternal life with God, no honor on earth can increase their happiness. In the hymn "Lead Me, Lord," John Becker has Jesus say, "Blessed are those whose hunger only holiness can fill, for I say they shall be satisfied." There is only one holiness (God's) though there are different ways of reflecting that holiness. Chapter five of

Vatican II's Dogmatic Constitution of the Church is entitled "The Universal Call to Holiness."

In his book *Married Saints* (Alba House), John Fink describes twenty-four married saints and their conjugal path to holiness. For over one thousand years the Catholic Church has had a Feast of All Saints, acknowledging that its list of saints can never account for everyone who is in heaven.

Saints point us to God. In February 2004, I visited Our Lady of the Angels Cathedral in Los Angeles and noticed that John Nava's tapestries (entitled "The Communion of Saints") presented one hundred and thirty-six people woven into twenty-five magnificent banners, all pointing toward the altar and the crucifix behind it.

These saints and blesseds include 124 who are named, plus twelve more infants, children, teens, and adults of various ethnic groups. Maria de la Cabeza and her husband, Isidore the Farmworker, are there as part of the "great cloud of witnesses" (see Hebrews 12:1) whom we hope to join at the eternal banquet.

Can People Communicate With the Dead?

What is the church's stand about people who claim to communicate with the dead? Is that like praying to saints? Or is it wrong? They are not claiming to foretell the future—only to communicate with deceased people.

Men and women who make their living by claiming to receive messages from dead people run the risk of violating the First Commandment—not to have any god besides the Lord.

The *Catechism of the Catholic Church* says, "All forms of *divination* are to be rejected: recourse to Satan or demons, conjuring up the dead or other practices falsely supposed to 'unveil' the future" (#2116).

The text continues: "Consulting horoscopes, astrology, palm reading, interpretation of omens and lots, the phenomena of clairvoyance, and recourse to mediums all conceal a desire for power over time, history, and, in the last analysis, other human beings, as well as a wish to conciliate hidden powers. They contradict the honor, respect, and loving fear that we owe to God alone."

Those who claim to communicate with the dead are not doing the equivalent of praying to saints. Few people claim to receive direct messages from saints—and for those who do so, such claims can never require belief or assent by anyone else.

Why Ask Saint Anthony's Help for Lost Objects?

Saint Anthony of Padua is associated with finding lost objects, but I have no idea why. What's the story behind this?

When Saint Anthony was preaching in southern France and teaching Scripture to the friars in Montpellier (1224–1227), a young Franciscan decided that he did not want to continue being a friar. He also stole the handwritten copy of the Psalms, the only one these Franciscans had. This rare and difficult-to-replace manuscript included Anthony's teaching notes.

On learning of the young man's departure and theft, knowing the time plus the expense of replacing that copy of the Psalms, Anthony prayed that the young man might have a change of heart. The young man returned the manuscript and resumed his life as a friar. Since then, people have been asking Anthony's help in finding lost objects.

Where Did Saint Francis Say That?

Saint Francis of Assisi is frequently credited as saying, "Preach the Gospel at all times. Use words if necessary." I have looked in several places but cannot find where he said this.

This is a great quote, very Franciscan in its spirit, but not literally from Saint Francis. The thought is his; the catchy phrasing is not in his writings or in the earliest biographies about him.

In Chapter XVII of his Rule of 1221, Francis told the friars not to preach unless they had received the proper permission to do so. Then he added, "Let all the brothers, however, preach by their deeds."

I had been a Franciscan for twenty-eight years—and had earned an M.A. in Franciscan studies—before I heard the "Use words if necessary" quote during Monsignor Kenneth Velo's homily at Cardinal Joseph L. Bernardin's funeral in 1996.

A few years after that, a friend of mine used the Internet to contact some of the most eminent Franciscan scholars in the world, seeking the source of the "Use words if necessary" quote. It is clearly not in any of Francis' writings. After a couple weeks of searching, no scholar could find this quote in a story written within two hundred years of Francis' death.

This saying and the "Peace Prayer," which Francis certainly did not write, are easily identified with him because they so thoroughly reflect his spirit. They probably would not have become so widespread if they were attributed to John Smith or Mary Jones.

The origins of the "Peace Prayer of Saint Francis" are thoroughly documented in Christian Renoux's 2001 book about the Peace Prayer. An eleventh-century French prayer is similar to the first part of the "Peace Prayer." The oldest known copy of the current prayer, however, dates to 1912 in France. The prayer became more well known in other countries during World War I.

This prayer is sold all over Assisi today—but always under the title "A Simple Prayer." Whoever linked it to Saint Francis guaranteed a wide diffusion of the text. The same is true for the "Use words if necessary" quote. Both reflect Saint Francis very well.

CHAPTER THREE

How We Read Scripture

What Does the Phrase "By Faith Alone" Mean?

As a Catholic, I have great difficulty in understanding Protestants who speak of salvation by faith alone. Does this come from differences between the King James Bible and Catholic translations of the Bible? Aren't there other parts of the Bible that explain salvation differently?

This, of course, was the subject of much misunderstanding during the Reformation in the sixteenth century. The expression "faith alone" is not found anywhere in the Bible's original Hebrew or Greek texts. Some people have mentally inserted this expression into Romans 1:17b ("[A]s it is written, 'The one who is righteous will live by faith'") and in related biblical passages.

The problem here is that "faith alone" could be understood as merely an activity of the mind. Someone could say: "I have faith; I am saved. My decisions no longer matter." It might have been to counteract such an interpretation of faith that Jesus clearly explains that saying "Lord, Lord" is not enough to be saved because people must do "the will of my Father in heaven" (Matthew 7:21). Matthew 25:31–46 and James 2:14–16 make for somber reading about the importance of a person's daily decisions. A living faith already includes a response to God's grace. John Feister's *Catholic Update* "How Catholics Understand Grace" explains how God's grace, human freedom, individual decisions, and salvation interact.

Can I Trust the Bible?

During a recent youth retreat at our parish, someone asked about Adam and Eve. Someone else said that it was just a story to explain how creation began and was not necessarily a real account. I always understood that the things in the Bible were inspired by God and were true. Now I am not so sure. What's going on here?

Yes, the Adam and Even account is a story, but a story full of meaning and truth. Both Jews and Christians accept this story as inspired by God.

If you had been present with a video camera at the creation of the world, would you have captured exactly what the book of Genesis describes? Would you have recorded *both* creation accounts (1:1—2:4a, as well as 2:4b–25)?

Not likely. These stories, however, convey powerful, fundamental, religious truths about human life. These stories are not written transcripts of videotaped recordings. Even a videotape is true from a limited *physical* perspective.

Was the final editor of the book of Genesis even saying that these stories are true in the same sense as a videotaped account? We have to respect the various kinds of writing that we find in the Bible, which is better described as a library of books by different human authors—all inspired by God.

In the ancient Near East, almost all creation stories, for example, denied that women were made from the same physical "stuff" as men. With its story about Adam's rib—a play on words in the original Hebrew—the book of Genesis tells us that God created men and women radically equal.

When you look at the daily newspaper, you expect that the stock market report will be accurate and that humor columns are indeed funny. A stock market report crafted to be funny is as useless as a tightly-reasoned humor column. You have to allow each type of writing to be what it is.

The book of Genesis is absolutely truthful about all creation's coming from a single source (God) and evil entering human life through a misuse of God-given freedom.

What Did God Mean?

As an eighth-grade religious education catechist, I will soon be using the story of Abraham's near-sacrifice of Isaac (Genesis 22:1–18) for a prayer service on faith. Over the years, I have struggled with the implications of this story and have found commentaries useful for adults. How can I present this to thirteen-year-olds? I fear that they will think that God delights in testing and tricking the people most loyal to him. If this is the kind of faith God demands, they may well ask, "Who needs it?"

Yes, this story is difficult to understand and to present. Yet it also plays an important part in forming Judeo-Christian ethics.

Why are we so repulsed by child sacrifice? In part, because *this* story tells us that the God of Abraham is not a God who wants that. In fact, some of the gods worshiped by Abraham's neighbors demanded child sacrifice!

The biblical God cannot do anything that contradicts what being God means. The story of Abraham's near-sacrifice of Isaac tells us that demanding child sacrifice would contradict what being God means. We abhor child sacrifice partially because this difficult story is in the Bible.

If your thirteen-year-olds react negatively to this story, you can initiate a discussion about today's more hidden child sacrifice (for example, abortions, child prostitution, or exploitation of children for work or military purposes.).

The fact that all these are done in the name of someone's freedom (not the child's!) does not legitimate any of them. Good luck in your challenging but absolutely essential ministry.

Why Should Christians Read the Old Testament?

My son, a sophomore at a Catholic high school, has a very hard time accepting the Old Testament in general. He believes many of the stories, beginning with the creation story and including Noah's ark, the parting of the Red Sea and others to be implausible as historical fact.

Frankly, I have some sympathy for his critique of the Old Testament. Still, other stories such as David's seem to have profound insight into the human condition and our relationship to God. How should I help my son sort this all out? I could use some help too.

Your son is finding his teen faith a little harder than that of his childhood. You are finding your adult faith more challenging than your teen faith. Both challenges are to be expected.

Your son's question involves history. Polytheism, belief in many gods, was presumed in the ancient world to be true. The Old Testament presents itself as God's self-revelation within human history. It helps us understand the one God and the divine plan for the world. The great danger was that the Hebrew people to whom the first revelation is directed might simply add the God of Abraham, Isaac, and Jacob to the other gods they knew. Biblical prophets constantly pointed out this danger. The New Testament continues God's self-revelation.

Is the Bible simply the written transcript of what your son might have captured if he had been present with a video camera during the events described? That is one type of reporting, what we tend to think of as the whole truth. Is the Bible, however, fundamentally God's unfolding self-revelation? That's where a more complete sense of truth is found, including meaning.

Take an example close to home. If your son asked you and your spouse to write out descriptions of when you got engaged, would you both include identical details? Even if you didn't, wouldn't the heart of both descriptions be true?

Let's apply this example to the creation story, cited by your son. In fact, the book of Genesis presents two creation accounts. The first one

(1:1–2:4a) describes the creation of the world in six days and God as resting on the Sabbath. The second one (starting at 2:4b) describes the creation of Adam and Eve in greater detail. These two accounts use different Hebrew words for God.

Because the final editor of the book of Genesis included both accounts, we must conclude that this editor understood them as telling us something very valuable about Creation—without either one being an eyewitness account. The world comes from a single source and not, as some pagan creation stories assert, the competition between a good god and an evil god.

Questions about the Bible's accuracy depend on recognizing what the Bible is (God's self-revelation in human history) and what it is not (an encyclopedia of science or a history book).

The introductions and notes in *The New American Bible* and in *The New Jerusalem Bible* are excellent and should help you and your son understand what the writers were doing in the stories about Noah's ark, the crossing of the Red Sea, and similar passages.

Your son finds the New Testament easier to understand and to accept than the Old Testament. OK, but God couldn't reveal everything at once. Belief in one God, for example, needed to be firm before the Incarnation or the Trinity could make sense. It helped that sacrifices in the Jerusalem Temple preceded Jesus' self-sacrifice on the cross.

God apparently wanted a group of monotheists to whom God's Son could break the news that God is truly Father, Son, and Holy Spirit—not three gods. God's covenant with the Jewish people has never been revoked and Christians cannot discard the Old Testament. God is the author of the entire Bible, even if God worked through many human writers.

Are the Old and New Testament Rules Different?

When I read the Old Testament, it seems to be highly "rules-based," unlike the New Testament, which strikes me as much more "spirit-based." Why is that?

Yes, there are many rules in the Old Testament, but there are also rules in the New Testament—just as God's spirit permeates both Testaments. Belief in one God was very much a minority position in the ancient world (see the previous Q&A). Pagan gods are pretty much like humans, for example, in terms of jealousy. These gods simply had more power to carry out their rivalries with other deities. Pagan gods expected an occasional sacrifice from their worshippers but very little in terms of moral conduct.

The God of Abraham, Isaac, and Jacob has a strong sense of justice and thus gives rules to ensure that the rights of all people are respected, especially groups such as widows and orphans (see the regulations in Deuteronomy 26).

Establishing and reinforcing belief in a single God was an uphill struggle; many Old Testament rules sought to help the Israelites make a clean break from the common wisdom of their pagan neighbors.

Christians no longer follow many Old Testament rules (such as the dietary laws, Temple sacrifices, and the obligation that males be circumcised) and have reinterpreted other rules (regarding Sunday instead of Saturday as the Lord's Day). Christians continue to follow the Ten Commandments and some other Old Testament rules.

The New Testament, however, has its share of rules. For example, the Last Judgment scene in Matthew 25:31–46 describes the need to feed the hungry, clothe the naked, and so on. In Luke 16:19–31, the rich man is condemned for ignoring the needs of Lazarus.

In Colossians 3:12–14, Saint Paul writes: "As God's chosen ones, holy and beloved, clothe yourselves with compassion, kindness, humility, meekness, and patience. Bear with one another and, if anyone has a complaint against another, forgive each other; just as the Lord has forgiven you, so you must also forgive. Above all, clothe yourselves with love, which binds everything together in perfect harmony."

Rules can protect relationships. In his book *Orthodoxy*, G.K. Chesterton writes, "If we wish to protect the poor we shall be in favor of fixed rules and clear dogmas. The *rules* of a club are occasionally in favour of the poor member. The drift of a club is always in favour of the rich one." Although following Jesus does not make us members of a club, I think Chesterton's observation describes why the New Testament includes rules.

One of the earliest heresies in Christianity is named after Marcion, a second-century Christian who felt the Old Testament and New Testament referred to very different gods—a justice-driven God vs. a mercy-driven God. Marcion also felt that the New Testament made the Old Testament superfluous.

Although Christians officially rejected these assertions, Marcion's objections have lived below the surface for many Christians. Such a viewpoint fails to recognize the Old and New Testaments as gifts from God.

Was the Old Covenant Cancelled?

Did Jesus' new covenant cancel the old one? If not, were Saint Peter and the apostles wrong in converting Jewish people to Christianity? Does the Catholic Church teach that salvation is possible without conforming to the New Covenant?

The Catholic Church teaches that salvation for anyone is possible only through the passion, death, and resurrection of Jesus Christ. Can only those people who have an explicit faith in Jesus Christ as the Son of God and their savior be saved? No.

Christianity has used an either/or approach only where absolutely necessary. Saint Paul addresses this issue in his letter to the Romans (chapters nine through eleven), noting that "the gifts and the calling of God are irrevocable" (11:29).

Saint Peter, the apostles, and their successors were not wrong in inviting Jewish men and women to an explicit belief in Jesus Christ. No one's salvation, however, is wholly dependent on whether he or she accepts baptism.

In article 1260, the *Catechism of the Catholic Church* teaches: "Since Christ died for all, and since all [people] are in fact called to one and the same destiny, which is divine, we must hold that the Holy Spirit offers to all the possibility of being made partakers, in a way known to God, of the Paschal mystery" [quoting *Gaudium et Spes*, Pastoral Constitution on the Church in the Modern World, 22].

The *Catechism* immediately states that everyone "who is ignorant of the Gospel of Christ and of his Church, but seeks the truth and does the will of God in accordance with his understanding of it, can be saved. It may be supposed that such persons would have *desired Baptism explicitly* if they had known its necessity."

Ultimately, only God's judgment about a person's salvation matters. To believe otherwise risks engaging in a subtle form of idolatry by substituting human judgment (always finite) for God's judgment (always complete).

Why Are Catholic and Protestant Bibles Different?

Why do Catholic Bibles have more books than Protestant Bibles like the King James Version or the New International Version? Why did the Catholics add books? Did some pope say to do that?

Seven Old Testament books are not found in the Old Testament section of the *King James Version* or other Protestant Bibles. These seven books were originally written in Greek or their Hebrew texts were no longer known in the late first century AD. During Jesus' lifetime, however, some Jewish people regarded these books as inspired by God. Some of the Gospels quote from or allude to these books.

About sixty years after Jesus' death, rabbis at Jamnia in Palestine drew up the list (canon) of the Scriptures used by Jewish people to this day. That shorter list includes only works composed in Hebrew, excluding the two books of Maccabees, the books of Wisdom, Judith, Tobit, Sirach, and Baruch, as well as parts of the books of Daniel and Esther.

For centuries, Eastern and Western Christians accepted the longer list as inspired; Roman Catholics and Orthodox Christians still do. When Martin Luther translated the Bible in the sixteenth century, he decided to use the shorter list.

Sometimes, these seven books are printed in Protestant Bibles under the heading "Deuterocanonical" or "Apocrypha." A 1546 decree from the fourth session of the Council of Trent affirmed the Catholic Church's use of the longer list, including the seven books and parts of two others.

Are There New Gospels?

I want to know more about the Gospel of Jesus that was found in 1945. Why are people hiding it from being released? I have not been very successful finding information on this. I have also heard about a Gospel of Thomas and a Gospel of Mary Magdalene.

I think you are referring to the Gospel of Thomas, one of three hundred Gnostic writings discovered in December 1945 at Nag Hammadi, Egypt. This writing exists completely only in the Coptic language; there are three fragments of it in Greek.

According to Anthony Saldarini in the *New Jerome Biblical Commentary*, of the 114 sayings of this Gospel (division made by modern scholars), seventy-nine of them have some parallel in the Gospels of Matthew, Mark, and Luke which, with the Gospel of John, are called "canonical." They belong to the *canon* or list of New Testament writings.

The Gospel of Thomas is called *apocryphal* because it is not in the New Testament. The Gospel of Mary Magdalene also belongs in this category.

Gnostics were people who relied on secret knowledge; *gnosis* is the Greek word for *knowledge*. Special teachers enabled Gnostics to hand on secret information not intended for everyone. In that general sense, Gnostics could be pagan, Jewish, or Christian. Scholars date the Gospel of Thomas to the start of the third century. It had a Gnostic final editor, at least.

Christian Gnostics claimed that Jesus wanted only a few of his followers to have the teachings they possessed. This knowledge was handed on by Gnostic teachers. The mainstream Christian community answered the Gnostic challenge by saying that Jesus intended bishops, successors of the apostles, as reliable teachers about him. They also said that the Christian community considered as inspired only the canonical books in the New Testament and the Old Testament.

The Scriptures were given to a faith community (Old Testament to the Jews, New Testament to Christians). They should be read with that in mind. If we trust those faith communities enough to tell us which writings are inspired by God, should we not also trust them to interpret them?

You may find these Gnostic Gospel texts, as well as more background, at your public library or through interlibrary loan.

Why Are There Four Gospels?

Does the church approve of attempts to combine the four Gospels? I know that the church did not approve the Diatesseron, *an early attempt to harmonize Matthew, Mark, Luke, and John. Was the objection to any attempt to combine them or to the fact that Tatian, who drew up the* Diatesseron, *later became a heretic? Is it dangerous for me to read a text combining four Gospels into a single account? What does the Catholic Church teach about this?*

Since my ancestors were Irish, I'll invoke the Irish prerogative of answering a question with another question—(three in fact!): Why is the possibility of harmonizing the four Gospels important to you? What would you gain from that? Do you find the present diversity of perspectives among the Gospel writers an obstacle to your faith?

The *Diatesseron* interweaves the four Gospels and two *non*-Gospel sources into a single text. It was completed around the middle of the second century and was probably written in Syriac. This text was certainly very influential in Syria and has been translated into many other languages.

The Catholic Church generally favors a both/and approach while employing an either/or position only when that is absolutely necessary.

The four canonical Gospels can easily look messy. Matthew's Gospel, for example, implies that Mary and Joseph lived in Bethlehem before Jesus' birth. Luke's Gospel clearly states they lived in Nazareth during that time period and only went to Bethlehem shortly before Jesus' birth. The *Diatesseron*'s approach allows one interpretation to prevail by silencing the other viewpoint.

Did Jesus heal a single blind man after leaving Jericho (Mark 10:46) or as he entered that city (Luke 18:35)? Or did he heal two blind men (Matthew 20:30–34)?

The *Diatesseron* is not so much a dangerous document as it is overconfident, tempting readers to believe that Tatian reconstructed events in a you-are-there way.

Harmonizing is important if you think of the Gospels as written transcriptions of videotapes recording the actual events. The church, however, does not understand them as that. People should take their lead on this from the faith community that recognizes *four* Gospels as inspired by God.

A book of Gospel parallels or cross-references for the four Gospels can be very helpful for study, but each Gospel's distinct personality must be recognized and respected. Some things work well in blenders; the Gospels do not.

Who Is James, Brother of the Lord?

Television shows and books refer to Saint James as the brother of Jesus. In the Apostles' Creed we say, "I believe in Jesus Christ, his only Son, our Lord...".

If Saint James is Jesus' brother, would James not also be God's son? Were Mary and Joseph the parents of James?

"James, the brother of the Lord" has puzzled people for centuries. The New Testament refers to three men named James.

James, brother of John the apostle, himself an apostle and a son of Zebedee (as in Matthew 4:21) is called James the Greater. He was martyred by King Herod Agrippa I about AD 41 (Acts 12:2) and is venerated at Santiago de Compostela, Spain.

James, son of Alphaeus, is also an apostle (mentioned in Matthew 10:3), known as James the Lesser. He was clubbed to death, according to one tradition, and is often confused with "James, the brother of the Lord."

The third James is the brother of Joseph/Joses, Simon, and Judas of Nazareth (Matthew 13:55, Mark 6:3). Jesus appeared to this James after the Resurrection (1 Corinthians 15:7). With Peter, he led the earliest Christian community in Jerusalem (Acts 12:17; 15:13–17), is mentioned by Saint Paul (Galatians 2:12), and was stoned to death in AD 62 on the high priest's orders.

This James is the presumed author of the New Testament Letter of James. He may have been Jesus' cousin; other members of his family headed the church in Jerusalem until that city was destroyed in AD 70.

For us, the term *brother* means a male relative sharing identical parents with the person who calls him "brother." In some societies, however, the term can include other male relatives, including cousins.

Jesus used *brother* in an even wider sense in Mark 3:35 ("Whoever does the will of God is my brother and sister and mother"), Matthew 25:40, Luke 22:32, and John 20:17.

The Catholic Church maintains that Mary had only one child, Jesus, who was not biologically the son of Joseph (Matthew 1:18–25 and Luke 1:34–35).

Already in the second century, the *Protoevangelium of James* described these "brothers of Jesus" as children of Joseph by a previous marriage.

Saint Jerome (d. 420) considered them cousins of Jesus. Matthew 13:56 and Mark 6:3 refer to Jesus' sisters but give no names.

There is no scriptural evidence that Joseph was a single parent before marrying Mary. Raymond Brown's *An Introduction to the New Testament* (Doubleday) has more on this subject.

Was That Woman Mary Magdalene?

Is the adulterous woman in John 8:1–11 Mary Madgalene?

The woman caught in adultery and then brought to Jesus is not Mary Magdalene. She is also not the "sinful woman" in Luke 7:36–50 or the woman who anointed Jesus a few days before his crucifixion (Matthew 26:6–13 and Mark 14:3–9).

Much is known for certain about Mary Magdalene: She helped finance Jesus and his disciples (Luke 8:2), had seven demons cast out of her (Mark 16:9 and Luke 8:2), and was present at the foot of the cross (implied in Luke 23:49 and listed in the other three Gospels). She is the only person all four Gospels agree saw the empty tomb on Easter morning and saw the Risen Jesus before any of the apostles did (Mark 16:9 and John 20:14–18). How ironic that she is remembered by many people for something that no Gospel says she did! And often not remembered for something that every Gospel says she did!

Mary Magdalene is probably associated with Luke's "sinful woman" story for two reasons: She is mentioned in the next story (8:1–3) and some Christians wanted a specific name for this penitent woman. In the Middle Ages, pilgrimages to her presumed relics at Vezelay in France were extremely popular because she was seen as the patron of all repentant sinners.

Based on internal evidence from John 8:1–11, many reputable Scripture scholars think that this story was not written by the author of that Gospel. It may have been inserted there by an editor who considered the story too important to risk losing.

Regardless of who wrote it, this account is as much a part of God's revelation as any other section of the Gospel of John.

What Belongs to Caesar?

I have never understood the passage where Jesus says that we should render to Caesar what is Caesar's and to God what is God's. How does the Catholic Church understand this passage?

The question this saying answered was posed by two groups with radically different political agendas, who were trying to trap Jesus on the question of whether it is legitimate to pay the census tax to Caesar (see Matthew 22:15–22). Although the Pharisees resented but grudgingly accepted Roman authority, the Herodians embraced Roman authority and prospered because of it. These rival groups joined forces to pose this question to Jesus, expecting it would force him into a lose-lose situation.

If he says yes, the Pharisees can denounce him as not being a good Jew. If he says no, the Herodians can accuse him of treason.

Jesus avoids this trap by asking to see the coin used to pay that tax. When they produce it rather easily, he observes that Caesar's image is on the coin. Some Jews in Palestine bitterly objected to using Roman coins, which bore the emperor's image. These Jews considered such coins a violation of the commandment against making graven images (Exodus 20:4 and Deuteronomy 5:8). The Jewish tax to support the Temple in Jerusalem, for example, could not be paid with Roman coins.

When Jesus says, "Then repay to Caesar what belongs to Caesar and to God what belongs to God," he is saying, in effect: "You have already bought into Caesar's system. Paying Caesar's taxes is part of that." The intended trap fails to ensnare Jesus.

Over the centuries, some Christians have understood this passage as suggesting that Caesar has some part of creation that God does not have. That cannot be; God created everything. What belongs to God and what belongs to Caesar are not two completely separate circles but rather a small circle (what belongs to Caesar) inside a much larger circle (what belongs to God).

This saying of Jesus neither advocates a separation of church and state nor says that the state has ultimate authority in all matters. Jesus reminded Pontius Pilate that only God has ultimate authority (John 19:11). Failing to remember that is a form of idolatry and invites a totalitarian form of government. In chapters thirteen, fourteen, seventeen, eighteen, and elsewhere, the book of Revelation criticizes the despotism of Roman emperors in the late first century AD.

Three hundred years later Saint Ambrose excommunicated the Emperor Theodosius who had ordered the massacre of seven thousand civilians in Thessalonika. Ambrose said, "The emperor is in the church, not above it." Theodosius repented.

Why Did Jesus Wash the Apostles' Feet?

According to the Gospel of John, at the Last Supper Jesus washed the feet of his apostles (13:1–11). This has always puzzled me. Why did Jesus do this?

The author of that Gospel provides the answer in the verses that immediately follow this event. Jesus asks his apostles, "Do you know what I have done to you? You call me Teacher and Lord—and you are right, for that is what I am. So if I, your Lord and Teacher, have washed your feet, you also ought to wash one another's feet. For I have set you an example, that you also should do as I have done to you. Very truly, I tell you, servants are not greater than their master, nor are messengers greater than the one who sent them. If you know these things, you are blessed if you do them" (John 13:12–17).

By washing the apostles' feet, Jesus links authority to humble service. This gesture explains servant leadership in an unforgettable way. This passage reinforces the teaching given when Jesus calls a child over after apostles ask, "Who is the greatest in the kingdom of heaven?" (Matthew 18:1) and replies, "Whoever becomes humble like this child is the greatest in the kingdom of heaven" (Matthew 18: 4). Luke's version of that incident appears in 9:46–48.

Jesus returns to this subject when the mother of James and John asks that her sons sit at Jesus' right and left in his kingdom (Matthew 20:27). Jesus contrasts authority as the pagans understand it and authority as his followers should view it. He says, "whoever wishes to be first among you must be your slave;…"

Many Christians have seen the washing of the apostles' feet as pointing to Jesus' supreme act of service when, on the cross, he cleansed us from sin.

We should be grateful that the foot-washing story was not lost; it is found only in the Gospel of John. Because the temptation to use authority for domination is so strong, we always need to hear Jesus' reminder that authority is for service.

Does the Gospel Address Social Issues?

Recently I have been reading about several twentieth-century Christians who applied Jesus' teaching to social issues. Is this essential to the gospel? Does the life and message of Jesus need to be embodied in new ways in each historical period?

The Good News of Jesus Christ affects all our relationships—with friends and family members but also our relationships with people whom we will never meet.

Jesus did not preach a privatized religion that influences only a fraction of someone's daily life. Anyone who tries to keep the Good News so tightly reined runs the risk of saying "Lord, Lord" but refusing to do God's will (see Matthew 7:21). When Jesus told the parable about the sheep and the goats at the Last Judgment (Matthew 25:31–46), Jesus taught that following him has implications for every relationship, for every attempt to reflect divine justice.

Social justice needs can evolve over time. There was no atomic bomb in Jesus' day. Does that mean the Good News has nothing to say about possessing nuclear weapons?

Slavery was much more common in Jesus' day than it is now. One reason it is not more common today is that Christians have recognized that "owning" people is not compatible with the Good News of Jesus. Every historical period contains social justice challenges for the followers of Jesus, who did not come so that his followers could separate people into who is worthy of God's love and who is not. He sought out many lost sheep.

In their final document, *Justicia in Mundo,* Justice in the World, participants at the 1971 World Synod of Bishops wrote: "Action on behalf of justice and participation in the transformation of the world fully appear to us as a constitutive dimension of the preaching of the Gospel, or, in other words, of the Church's mission for the redemption of the human race and its liberation from every oppressive situation" (Introduction).

One of the *Eucharistic Prayers for Masses for Various Needs and Occasions* addresses God by saying: "Open our eyes to the needs of all; inspire us with words and deeds to comfort those who labor and are burdened; keep our service of others faithful to the example and command of Christ.

"Let your Church be a living witness to truth and freedom, to justice and peace, that all people may be lifted up by the hope of a world made new."

Jesus' followers do not always live up to this, but the Good News tells us that we must allow our following of Jesus to influence every relationship.

Although there may be legitimate differences of opinion among Christians regarding specific strategies to correct social injustices, Jesus' followers cannot ignore such differences by saying that religion is private and has no role in public life. Jesus always invites us to live out our baptism in honest, persevering, and generous ways.

CHAPTER FOUR

How We Celebrate the Sacraments

Is There a Right to the Sacraments?

Our archdiocese has several priestless parishes and is looking at many more within a few years. Deacons, religious, and laypeople are being prepared to take over as administrators. That's fine—but laypeople cannot normally preside at weddings and deacons cannot celebrate Mass, hear confessions, or anoint the sick.

In view of the obligation to participate in Sunday Mass and to confess mortal sins at least once a year, I am starting to wonder: Do laypeople have a right to the sacraments? Might that require bishops to ordain married men as priests?

I know that some people argue that changing the celibacy rule involves many other issues, for example, financial support. Do practical challenges constitute a theological/doctrinal reason to reserve access to the sacraments to a small percentage of people living close to a priest? If the faithful have a right to the sacraments, is it moral to withhold access to the sacraments because of a man-made rule?

People have a right to receive the sacraments for which they are properly prepared. Speaking about a "right to the sacraments," however, does not mean that all preparation for them can be waived because every baptized Catholic already has an absolute right to each sacrament.

Every Catholic certainly has a right to access to the sacrament of reconciliation. On the other hand, there is no question that the church has a right to do its best to make sure that parents preparing for the baptism of a child, couples preparing for marriage, children preparing for First Communion, and candidates for holy orders are properly prepared.

Bishops seek to provide for the sacramental needs of the people entrusted to them by encouraging vocations to ordained ministry as priests or permanent deacons. At times, bishops of a certain region on their *ad limina* visit to the pope have sought permission to ordain married men to the priesthood. It has not been granted.

The practice of ordaining as Catholic priests some men who previously served as Protestant ministers or Anglican priests indicates that celibacy is not an absolute requirement for ordination in the Catholic Church. Even so, the Latin rite of the Catholic Church has chosen to maintain this custom.

In many parts of Central and South America, as well as Africa, bishops have designated catechists or "ministers of the Word" to lead prayer services and distribute Holy Communion. That is not the same as a Mass, of course, but this practice means that people have greater access to the Eucharist than they otherwise would.

Are Sacraments Performed By Sinful Priests Valid?

If a priest is not in the state of grace when he baptizes someone, hears confession, celebrates Mass, anoints a sick person, or officiates at a marriage, is that sacrament valid? What if some bishop or archbishop is not in the state of grace when he confirms or ordains someone?

In the early fourth century, a North African bishop named Donatus contested the election of Caecilian as bishop of Carthage, saying that he had denied the faith under persecution and therefore could no longer celebrate sacraments validly. Even though a synod in Rome in AD 313 formally rejected this teaching of Donatus, the controversy remained very much alive for another century.

Although the church wants its priests and bishops to be in a state of grace (as it wants the same for all followers of Jesus), the church denies that a sacrament's validity depends on the holiness of the priest, bishop, or the layperson (in the case of marriage or emergency baptism) who is its minister.

The authorized person must perform the action, say the prescribed words and "intend to do what the church does" in this sacrament. Saint Augustine of Hippo addressed this issue in his famous work *Concerning Baptism*. The Donatist position, in fact, casts doubt on the validity of every celebration of each sacrament. The church rejected the teaching of Donatus, who died around AD 350.

The priest, deacon, couple to be married, or layperson performing an emergency baptism—all of these should be in the state of grace when they celebrate the sacraments. That is not required, however, for sacraments to work.

The *Catechism of the Catholic Church* teaches, "From the moment that a sacrament is celebrated in accordance with the intention of the Church, the power of Christ and his Spirit acts in an through it, independently of the personal holiness of the minister. Nevertheless, the fruits of the sacraments also depend on the disposition of the one who receives them" (#1128).

The Catholic church wants the ministers of God's sacraments to be in the state of grace when they act in its name. But requiring this for the sacrament to work opens all sacramental celebrations to doubt regarding their validity. This further suggests that human sin can overpower God's grace. Not so, regarding the sacrament of penance or any other sacrament.

A priest conscious of not being in the state of grace should try to receive the sacrament of reconciliation as soon as possible. If he is not able to do so, he should try to make a perfect act of contrition, celebrate the sacrament in question, and then seek absolution as soon as he is able.

All the church's members need to cooperate generously with God's grace—and thus become holy!

Can a Divorced Person Still Receive the Sacraments?

I am a Catholic. My wife and I divorced seven years ago. I attend church periodically but pray almost daily. In talking with other Catholics, if the subject of my divorce comes up, they cut the conversation short.

Am I prevented from receiving any sacraments? Is an annulment necessary for continuing my life as a Catholic? If so, would that render my son illegitimate?

If you have not remarried and are properly disposed, you can receive the sacraments of confirmation, Eucharist, penance, or anointing of the sick.

A declaration of nullity, sometimes called an annulment, says that you are free to marry within the church or that an existing civil marriage can be convalidated (regularized).

Declarations of nullity do not render children illegitimate because the church presumes that the bride and groom married in good faith. That marriage was valid in civil law even if it is later declared not to be a valid sacramental marriage.

Is Infant Baptism in the Bible?

Why do Catholics baptize babies? It seems quite obvious to me that you have to be an adult in order to follow Jesus. Where does the Bible say that babies should be baptized?

In Philippi, Saint Paul baptized his jailer "and all his family" (Acts 16:33). That does not prove that children were included, but it seems possible, even likely. In Ephesians 6:1–3 we read: "Children, obey your parents in the Lord for this is right. Honor your father and mother— this is the first commandment with a promise: so that it may be well with you and you may have a long life on earth."

Saint Paul also writes, "Children, obey your parents in everything, for this is your acceptable duty in the Lord" (Colossians 3:20). Why would Saint Paul write advice to children if they were not considered part of the church?

The strongest biblical evidence for baptizing children is probably Matthew 19:13–15. "Then children were being brought to him in order that he might lay his hands on them and pray. The disciples spoke sternly to those who brought them, but Jesus said, 'Let the children come to me, and do not stop them; for it is to such as these that the kingdom of heaven belongs.' After he laid his hands on them and went on his way."

The Greek verb *koluein*, translated as "not prevent," was earlier used in Mark 10:14 and in Luke 18:16 in the same baptismal context. It appears again in Acts 8:36 when the Ethiopian eunuch asks, "What is to prevent me from being baptized?" This verb is used again when Peter is ready to baptize the Roman centurion Cornelius (Acts 10:47) and when Peter later justifies that decision (11:17). Is all this a coincidence? Maybe, maybe not.

The Introduction for the *Rite of Baptism for Children* quotes John 3:5 ("No one can enter the kingdom of God without being born of water and Spirit" (NRSV)) and then comments: "The Church has always understood these words to mean that children should not be deprived of Baptism, because they are baptized in the faith of the Church, a faith proclaimed for them by their parents and godparents, who represent both the local Church and the whole society of saints and believers: 'The whole Church is the mother of all and the mother of each' [St. Augustine of Hippo].

"To fulfill the true meaning of the sacrament, children must later be formed in the faith in which they have been baptized. The foundation of this formation will be the sacrament itself that they have already received. Christian formation, which is their due, seeks to lead them gradually to learn God's plan in Christ, so that they may ultimately accept for themselves the faith in which they have been baptized" (#2–3).

The church has baptized children since the time of Jesus. Was it mistaken about this for another fifteen centuries until some Protestant reformers challenged this practice? I doubt that.

Consciously or unconsciously, parents are always passing on values to their children. Why shouldn't they pass on their faith? To insist that only adults can be baptized risks the heresy of Pelagianism, which said that human effort matters most regarding a person's salvation.

Every baptized person needs to mature in his or her faith. If the church baptized only adults, that would almost guarantee a false sense of security, a conviction that ongoing conversion is no longer necessary. That is not the Good News that Jesus preached. Only in heaven will Jesus' followers have "arrived."

What Is Required to Become a Godparent?

What are the requirements for being a godparent? Must both of them be Catholic? Must there be a man and a woman? Can you change godparents later if the first ones fail to be good role models?

Canon 874, #1 of the present *Code of Canon Law* says that the person selected must:

> be appointed by the person to be baptized, his/her parents or the parish priest and be suitable for the role and have the intention of fulfilling it,

> be at least sixteen years old unless the local bishop sets a different age or the parish priest considers that there is a just reason for an exception,

> be a Catholic, be confirmed and made his or her First Communion and "lives a life of faith which befits the role to be undertaken,"

> not be under any canonical penalty, and

> not be the father or mother of the person to be baptized.

Canon 874, #2, indicates that at least one of the godparents must be a Catholic. In fact, only one godparent is required (Canon 873).

When there are two godparents, they need to be a man and a woman so that the newly baptized will have a role model for each gender. Should the original sponsors later turn out not to be good role models in Catholic faith, the best solution is to find better role models and involve them more closely in the baptized person's life. Under some circumstances, records at the parish where a baptism is registered can be changed. Doing that, however, will change little unless better role models have already been identified.

William Wegher's *Catholic Update* "Godparents and Sponsors: What Is Expected of Them Today?" can be read at www.American Catholic.org.

Can I Baptize My Great-grandchildren?

My three grandsons are all unmarried but are living with young women and have children. I have several friends who share a similar heartache. They tell me that they have sprinkled each one and baptized them. Can I do this?

I understand the heartache that your great-grandchildren have not been baptized, but I cannot advise you to baptize them secretly, without their parents' knowledge or permission.

Unbaptized children can be saved (see *Catechism of the Catholic Church*, #1261). When the church baptizes an infant, it asks parents or those presenting the child about their willingness to raise the child as a Catholic. If that readiness does not exist, the priest may decline celebrating the sacrament of baptism then.

You may have expected me to give a different answer. Please do not underestimate the power of your good example. Children are sometimes more influenced by the faith of grandparents (great-grandmother in your case) than by their parents' apparent lack of faith.

How Can I Become Catholic?

I am interested in becoming a Catholic, but I don't know where to start. Because I don't have any good friends who are Catholic, the thought of call-

ing up a Catholic parish and stating my interest is pretty intimidating. Is there anything on the Internet that can help me get started?

Whether you have been baptized already or not, becoming a Catholic is a process of discernment and preparation. The Rite of Christian Initiation of Adults (RCIA) prepares the unbaptized for baptism in the Catholic Church; it also prepares those already baptized in another church for "reception into full communion with the Catholic Church." Most parishes have an RCIA group that usually begins in the fall and concludes with Easter in the spring. Participants receive instruction and learn how to share in the faith life of that parish. You can find the parish nearest you through www.MassTimes.org.

In the *Catholic Update* archives section at www.American Catholic.org, you will find over two hundred links to past issues. You may want to start with any link that has RCIA in its title; many others will also be helpful.

Best wishes for your continuing faith journey!

Why Does Confession Seem So Threatening?

Confession has been a really sore spot for me but, having been raised a Catholic, I do love the church and its other sacraments. I am sure there are priests I could go to for confession, but I feel so uncomfortable and always feel that God already knows my sins and what I am sorry for. Will I go to hell for feeling this way? Will God forgive me if I am truly sorry?

You will not go to hell for feeling that way—only if you commit some mortal sin for which you refuse to repent. Will God forgive you if you are truly sorry? Yes.

You may, however, be seeing repentance and forgiveness too narrowly. Sin cuts us off not only from God but also from other people. Repentance is not simply about straightening things out with an angry God who, in human terms, is actually more disappointed than angry.

Repentance is also about admitting that our sins affect how we treat other people. The Roman Catholic faith is an incarnational one, a sacramental one, a faith which sees God acting through physical objects (water, oil, bread, wine) and by means of human instruments, including a priest hearing confessions.

Why not participate in an Advent or Lent penance service in your parish? Common prayers and Scripture readings are followed by a chance for private confession in the open or in a confessional.

In more than thirty-five years of hearing confessions, I have always been humbled and edified as people face their sinfulness, accepting God's love and forgiveness. Remember, confessors go to confession, too!

When Are My Sins Forgiven?

When I say the Act of Contrition, are my sins taken away immediately? Or is my prayer simply a request that God in his mercy will grant forgiveness— as in the sacrament of penance?

God knows each person's heart and thus forgives when God knows that we are truly sorry for our sins. As part of that forgiveness, God counts on us to do all that we can to repair the damage that our sins have caused.

If we say we are sorry for our sins but then want to consider every-thing settled, we are not taking sin seriously enough. We risk living in an illusion.

God knows that no amount of contrition can, by itself, undo sin's damage. Thus, the Act of Contrition that we pray during the sacrament of reconciliation is *part* of this sacrament, not a substitute for it. God rightly expects us to work toward mitigating the damage that our sins have caused.

Sin disrupts our relationship with God but also with other people. If I tell a lie about my next-door neighbor, my lie affects both God and that neighbor. I cannot cut a deal with God and ignore the fact that my sins always have consequences beyond what I may expect or would like them to have. Every sin has a life of its own, a life that I need to face whenever I seek forgiveness.

Sin tends to confuse our sense of what is public and what is private. Our temptation is always to consider sin as affecting only our relationship with God.

Every sin claims to open up our world, but each one actually shuts it down in some way. Auxiliary Bishop Robert Morneau of Green Bay, Wisconsin, wrote in *The Compass* (the diocesan newspaper) in 2009: "Sin leads to blindness, darkness and death. One example would be that of greed. When this capital sin takes over, we can no longer see what really matters. All of one's passion is directed to the acquisition of more and more. Sin fosters self-preoccupation and a cramped life." Bishop Morneau recalled that Saint Augustine of Hippo once described sin as "a turning in on oneself."

Like Adam and Eve, we are tempted to point to others if someone questions us about our sins. The book of Genesis indicates that sin's first casualty was a sense of personal responsibility. God-given freedom is often exchanged for a glittering form of slavery.

We are constantly tempted to regard sin as the most natural thing in the world while viewing virtue, sin's opposite, as something that requires superhuman effort on our part. Nothing could be further from the truth! We are "wired" for virtue, to cooperate with God's grace.

While encouraging you to keep praying the Act of Contrition, I also suggest that you use this prayer to help you repair whatever damage your sins have caused. There is always more to repair than we are inclined to admit.

How Often Is Confession Required?

When must I receive the sacrament of reconciliation? My parish bulletin recently listed "Go to confession at least once a year" under the heading "Precepts of the Church." My understanding has always been that confession is required in the case of mortal sin, regardless of the interval since the previous time, and that it is not absolutely required otherwise. Is that correct?

Yes, it is. The Fourth Lateran Council issued a decree in 1215 that each Catholic should receive the sacrament of penance at least once a year if the person is conscious of having committed a mortal sin since his or her last confession. This was reaffirmed at the Council of Trent.

According to Canon 989 of the Western Church's *Code of Canon Law,* "All the faithful who have reached the age of discretion are bound faithfully to confess their grave sins at least once a year."

The church, however, continues to recommend highly that we bring venial sins to confession. Section 1458 of the *Catechism of the Catholic Church* teaches:

> Without being strictly necessary, confession of everyday faults (venial sins) is nevertheless strongly recommended by the Church. Indeed the regular confession of our venial sins helps us form our conscience, fight against evil tendencies, let ourselves be healed by Christ and progress in the life of the Spirit. By receiving more frequently through this sacrament the gift of the Father's mercy, we are spurred to be merciful as he is merciful....

The example of many saints confirms the truth of this teaching. To some extent, every sin redefines our sense of what is normal, what is growing within our lives. Regular confession helps us to ask the question, "Are the right things growing in my life?" Regular confession can help us avoid the slippery slope of describing everything that seems to our advantage as "no big deal."

How Are Sunday and Weekday Readings Selected?

Who decides the readings used at Sunday Mass? Sometimes the reading begins a story, skips several verses and then continues the story. Why? What do Year I and Year II mean regarding the weekday readings?

Our three-year cycle of Sunday readings uses Matthew in Year A, Mark in Year B, and Luke in Year C, starting with the First Sunday of Advent.

The Gospel of John is used each year during the Easter season and during Year B because the Gospel of Mark is shorter than the others.

The Sunday Gospel readings were chosen first; the First Reading is coordinated with it. The Second Reading is continuous from the previous Sunday, almost always on a different theme.

Weekday Masses have a single cycle of Gospel readings, using all four Gospels each year. The first weekday reading is either Year I (odd-numbered years) or Year II (even-numbered years). The weekday readings are the same for the Advent, Christmas, Lent, and Easter seasons. Feasts and solemnities have their own readings. Some Protestant churches use the same lectionary as Roman Catholics use, though translations may vary.

A reading can omit a few verses. This usually provides greater clarity but can raise problems about context.

Does TV Mass Count?

If you watch Mass on TV, does that count as going to Mass on Sunday?

The church allows the Mass to be televised primarily for the benefit of those in hospitals, nursing homes, or people confined to their own homes. Televised Masses also enable people around the world to participate in some way in papal Masses for Christmas, Easter, World Youth Day, and other special events such as the funeral of Pope John Paul II, or the Mass during which Pope Benedict XVI was installed in his ministry as pope, etc.

Someone who is well enough to go to Mass on Sunday, however, cannot fulfill his or her obligation to participate in Mass by choosing to stay home and watch a TV Mass. Why not? That would be privatizing what should be a *community* celebration. Vatican II's *Sacrosanctum Concilium*, Constitution on the Sacred Liturgy, calls for "full, conscious and active participation" in the Mass (#14). If you could go but choose not to, you are not participating fully.

By baptism, we become members of the church. Through directly sharing in the Eucharist, our baptismal identity is reinforced and our conversion to God's ways is deepened.

We *become* church by *praying* as church.

Is Receiving Communion in the Hand Sacrilegious?

A friend of mine, a daily communicant, says that receiving Holy Communion in the hand is sacrilegious. When I told my sister this, she asked, "How did the apostles receive Holy Communion at the Last Supper?"

Receiving Holy Communion in the hand was approved as an option by the United States bishops in May 1977, confirmed by the Holy See and officially introduced that fall. Episcopal conferences in most other countries have given similar approval.

On June 14, 2001, the United States bishops approved *Norms for the Distribution and Reception of Holy Communion Under Both Kinds in the Dioceses of the United States of America.*

Section 41 reads: "Holy Communion under the form of bread is offered to the communicant with the words, 'The Body of Christ." The communicant may choose whether to receive the Body of Christ in the hand or on the tongue. When receiving in the hand, the communicant should be guided by the words of Saint Cyril of Jerusalem: 'When you approach, take care not to do so with your hand stretched out and your fingers open or apart, but rather place your left hand as a throne beneath your right, as befits one who is about to receive the King. Then receive him, taking care that nothing is lost.'"

According to Section 160 of the 2002 *General Instruction of the Roman Missal*, "When receiving Holy Communion standing, the communicant bows his or her head before the sacrament as a gesture of reverence and receives the Body of the Lord from the minister. The consecrated host may be received either on the tongue or in the hand at the discretion of each communicant."

Your friend, a daily communicant, is free to receive Holy Communion on the tongue but certainly cannot describe as sacrilegious what the church has officially approved.

Unfortunately, some Catholics tend to condemn for others what they choose not to do themselves. In this way, they risk turning Christ's sacrament of unity into a sacrament of division. In 1 Corinthians 11:17–34, Saint Paul rebukes those Christians for making the Eucharist a sign of division.

We do not know how the apostles received Holy Communion at the Last Supper, but I suspect that your sister is correct that it was in the hand. May all of us cooperate generously with the grace of that sacrament!

Can I Receive Communion in a Protestant Church?

I recently attended the wedding of a friend's son in a Protestant ceremony. During the Communion service I received Communion to show respect for my friend and his son. Afterward, I questioned if I should have done that. How does the Catholic Church view this situation?

The Catholic Church does not see this as proper because the physical act of receiving Communion is virtually the same during a Catholic Mass and a service such as this one. The faith represented by everyone who received Communion at that wedding is not the same, however. What you believe about the Eucharist differs from what that faith community officially teaches about the presence of Jesus in the Eucharist.

Your desire to honor your friend and his son is commendable, but should that come at the cost of obscuring what you believe about the Eucharist? If you go to www.AmericanCatholic.org, you can find our *Catholic Update* "Real Presence in the Eucharist."

The *Catechism of the Catholic Church* teaches that Eucharistic intercommunion with ecclesial communities derived from the Reformation is not possible because of the absence of the Sacrament of Holy Orders. The *Catechism* goes on to teach: "However these ecclesial communities, 'when they commemorate the Lord's death and resurrection in the holy Supper...profess that it signifies life in communion with Christ and await his coming in glory'" (# 1400, citing *Unitatis redintegratio*, Decree on Ecumenism, 3).

Some day intercommunion may represent a common belief in the sacrament of the Eucharist, but at present it does not. This issue is openly addressed in various ecumenical dialogues.

Why Do We Pray for the Deceased?

Who do we celebrate Masses for people who have died? When did this custom begin? What can you tell me about its spread?

I cannot give you an exact date for the first time this happened. It was a natural step from remembering martyrs to remembering other holy people to remembering those who may need further purification. There are prayers for the dead in the Third Anaphora of Saint Peter (Sharar) used by the Maronite Church today; that text dates to AD 431.

The Mass links us to the all the living, all the saints and "all the dead whose faith only you [God] can know" (Eucharistic Prayer for Masses for Various Needs and Occasions).

In book nine of the *Confessions*, Saint Augustine of Hippo describes extended conversations with his mother, Saint Monica, shortly before her death in AD 387. He reports that she asked him to remember her during celebrations of the Mass.

Can Masses Be Offered for Non-Catholics?

At our parish, a Sunday Mass was recently offered for a non-Catholic couple. Is that allowed?

Canon 901 of the 1983 *Code of Canon Law* states, "A priest is entitled to offer Mass for anyone, living or dead." The commentary of the Canon Law Society of Great Britain and Ireland notes, "Canons 1184–1185 forbid a funeral Mass for certain people, but this would not prevent a priest saying Mass for these people. Prudence might have to be exercised in publicly announcing such Mass intentions."

Canon 1184 lists three categories of persons to whom church funerals are to be denied unless they gave some signs of repentance before death: notorious apostates, heretics, and schismatics; those who for anti-Christian motives chose that their bodies be cremated; and other manifest sinners to whom a church funeral could not be granted without public scandal to the faith. The same canon notes that the bishop of the diocese is to be consulted if any doubt occurs.

Your letter did not indicate that the people you mentioned belong in any of those three categories. The publicized Mass intention was proper.

Can Ashes Be Scattered?

I understand the church's regulations on cremation. What are the church's regulations about the final disposition of a deceased person's ashes?

The church expects entombment of ashes in a conventional grave, a mausoleum or a *columbarium* (cemetery niche for the container). The *Order of Christian Funerals* approved for the dioceses of the United States by the United States Conference of Catholic Bishops and the Holy See contains an alternate prayer for cremated remains. That prayer begins, "My friends, as we prepare to bury (entomb) the ashes of our brother (sister)...." Later it continues, "Comfort us today with the words of your promise as we return the ashes of our brother (sister) to the earth."

The *Guidelines for Christian Burial in the Catholic Church*, prepared by the Liturgy Advisory Committee of the National Catholic Cemetery Conference, state, "Unless otherwise directed by the diocesan bishop, the cremated remains should never be scattered or disposed of in any manner other than a dignified interment or entombment."

Burial at sea is permitted for a body or a person's ashes. Federal law prohibits such burials less than three nautical miles from land.

Is Confirmation Required Before Marriage?

In order for a person to be married in the Catholic Church, does he or she have to be confirmed first?

The *Code of Canon Law*, the basic law of the Roman Catholic Church, says, "Catholics who have not yet received the Sacrament of Confirmation are to receive it before being admitted to marriage, if this can be done without grave inconvenience" (Canon 1065, #1).

If a Catholic approaches his or parish at least six months before the wedding—as many dioceses ask—that should provide ample time to make the necessary preparations for confirmation.

Regarding resources about church law, I recommend *New Commentary on the Code of Canon Law* (Paulist). It was edited by John Beal, James Coriden, and Thomas Green. *Surprised by Canon Law: 150 Questions Catholic Ask about Canon Law* (Servant), by Pete Vere and Michael Trueman may also be helpful.

In What Faith Should We Raise Our Children?

My fiancé is Methodist and I am Catholic. We are both very happy in our religions; neither of us wants to convert. I was raised in a Catholic school, and it is important to me to be married in the Catholic Church. I want to raise our children as Catholics but he wants them to be raised in both religions. What can we do?

Your future children can be raised to *respect* both religions but they can hardly be genuine *members* of both.

Consider, for example, the Catholic teaching about the Eucharist. Even though a child could be presented with the Catholic teaching about it (real presence of Jesus) and the Methodist teaching about it (memorial presence), that child cannot simultaneously commit to such divergent teachings. One must prevail.

Catholics recognize the sacrament of penance and Methodists do not. Catholics see the pope as exercising a ministry entrusted to the Apostle Peter; Methodists do not. A child cannot be raised in two religious traditions in all respects.

Our *Catholic Update* "Interchurch Marriages: How to Help Them Succeed" can be read at www.AmericanCatholic.org.

Why Celebrate Weddings in Churches?

I have always dreamed of an outdoor wedding. I recently told my aunt that I wanted to get married outdoors and how romantic I thought it would be. She said that the church does not consider a couple married unless they are married in a church building. Is this true?

Although this issue arises in terms of *where* the ceremony will occur, I suspect the much deeper issues include: What does this marriage represent? Is faith in Jesus important to the bride and groom? Is this marriage a statement of faith—as well as a statement of undertaking new civil obligations?

Although your aunt may have overstated the case (exceptions are possible), most, if not all, Roman Catholic dioceses in the United States require the bishop's permission for a wedding celebrated outside a church building.

This "dispensation from form" is more readily given if one of the spouses is not baptized. Having a wedding in a church can imply something that is simply not true for this couple. If both spouses are Christian, a church building can remind the guests that the faith community has a stake in the success of this marriage.

Although weddings reflect the personal preferences and cultural backgrounds of the couple, they are not, strictly speaking, private celebrations because marriages have major consequences for the church and for civil society.

At a wedding, a Catholic priest or deacon is the church's representative. He is not employed by the couple in the same way that they hire florists, dressmakers, musicians, photographers, caterers, or others.

Because a Catholic couple is preparing to enter a marriage in the Lord, the ceremony needs to reflect the church's understanding of this sacrament and the preparation needed for it.

Marriage is a lifelong commitment, which the larger faith community has a responsibility to nurture. Linking weddings to buildings used by the faith community is one way of making that point. Weddings are usually celebrated in church buildings for the same reasons that baptisms are celebrated there: That is where the faith community most often gathers.

Once you move weddings out of a church building, you face potential questions about having them on a roller coaster or Ferris wheel, while scuba diving, or in some other location that the couple considers ideal. I have read news reports about weddings in all these places. How do such locations favor or discourage participation by the larger faith community?

That community certainly has a stake in the success of every marriage its members enter. Should problems arise in a marriage, will the husband and wife turn only to those who witnessed their exchange of vows?

Please check with your parish priest to learn the regulations in your diocese regarding the site of weddings.

In the course of their marriage, a couple may change parishes several times, but the church proposes the local parish as the usual place for weddings because *some* local parish will presumably be part of their marriage in the Lord.

According to one saying, "A wedding is for a day. A marriage is for a lifetime." Best wishes for a beautiful wedding ceremony, followed by a long and faith-filled marriage.

Why Does the Church Have Annulments?

As a Catholic who married young, then divorced, and has since remarried, I don't understand why the Catholic Church makes it so difficult for divorced Catholics to come back to the sacraments.

Why can't I confess this, be forgiven, and then be received back into the church without going through all that horrible paperwork that peeks into your very personal life? I want to receive Holy Communion again and fill the hole in my life that the church once filled.

The Catholic Church's practice regarding divorced and remarried Catholics and the Eucharist reflects three basic beliefs: 1) the decision to marry is the most important lifelong decision that most people ever make; 2) some marriages that appear to be valid, sacramental marriages (the kind that can be dissolved only by death) are, in fact, not that; and 3) it is good for Catholic couples to grow together within valid, sacramental marriages.

Respect for marriage has led the Catholic Church to establish marriage tribunals to determine whether a now-divorced couple ever had a valid, sacramental marriage. If not, each may be able to enter such a marriage with someone else.

Tribunals must work on the basis of evidence, usually given by deposition but sometimes given in person. Marriage is a public act, with public consequences, regardless of whether that couple had children or not. The marriage partner who did not initiate the annulment is called "the respondent" and has specific rights during the annulment process.

"All that horrible paperwork," as you call it, aims to establish whether there was ever a valid, sacramental marriage. Is it possible that someone has exaggerated to you the difficulty of this process? Some people who have gone through this process have found it a healing experience.

Can a Civil Marriage Be Convalidated?

Reader #1: I was married in a government office and divorced four years later. My present marriage of eighteen years was also conducted in a government office. I am Catholic; however, my husband has no faith association at all. Is there any hope for my marriage situation? Is there a procedure whereby I can become right with the church?

Reader #2: I am interested in finding out how to reenter the Catholic Church. I was baptized and confirmed as a Catholic. However, when I married my husband, the ceremony was performed by a justice of the peace. My husband was baptized and received his First Communion but was never con-firmed as a Catholic. We have not attended church for roughly ten years; our three children have not been baptized. I would like to know the steps I need to take to have my children baptized and for my family to begin attending Mass and receiving the sacraments.

Thanks to both of you for writing and for seeking to reestablish your-selves as Catholics. A religious identity that might not seem terribly important at the time of a wedding can later matter greatly to a spouse. *Convalidation* is name for the process by which the Catholic Church officially recognizes a marriage previously valid only in civil law or rec-ognized there and by some non-Catholic religion. Convalidation is a new act of marriage consent, one now officially recognized by the Catholic Church. The consent must be exchanged before a priest or deacon, with at least two other witnesses.

Reader #1, your first marriage was probably not a sacramental one because, as a Catholic, you were bound by "canonical form" (to marry before a priest, deacon, or someone previously designated by the Catholic Church to witness that marriage). If your ex-spouse is no longer living, you are certainly free to convalidate your civil marriage.

If you have been married only twice, it should be possible for a dioce-san tribunal, which handles marriages cases, to issue a declaration of nullity because of "lack of canonical form." This will require official copies of your baptismal record, your marriage record (not the marriage license), and your divorce decree.

You must arrange for this declaration of nullity (commonly known as an annulment) through a parish. Once it has been given, then you and your parish priest or deacon can schedule a time for the convalidation (assuming that the Catholic Church would consider your present hus-band free to marry you. For example, that he has no ex-wife living, is not your first cousin, or is prevented by some other marriage imped-iment).

If your present husband has never been baptized, you will need a dispensation called "disparity of cult." Your parish can obtain it quite easily.

Reader #2, you have a simple case—assuming that neither you nor your husband was ever married before and are not prevented by some other impediment from marrying each other now. Both you and your husband were bound by "canonical form" and probably did not have the church's permission to be married by a justice of the peace. After you approach a parish priest and explain your situation, you need to obtain copies of your respective baptismal records and an official copy of your marriage record. Then you can arrange for a convalidation.

Reader #2, your husband should make arrangements to receive the sacrament of confirmation. Depending on the ages of your children, they can be baptized immediately or after receiving appropriate instruction.

At www.AmericanCatholic.org, readers can find our February 2004 article about convalidation. Sister Victoria Vondenberger's book, *Catholics, Marriage and Divorce: Real People, Real Questions* (St. Anthony Messenger Press) explains declarations of nullity and other marriage tribunal processes that may be necessary for a convalidation.

Can an Ex-Spouse Veto an Annulment?

In college, my husband married a young woman in a non-Catholic church. After he discovered her infidelity, they divorced. Ten years later when we were planning to marry, we were told that he had to get an annulment but to do that his ex-wife would have to sign a document giving him permission to remarry. Because I couldn't expect him to track down this woman and ask her to sign such a document, we married in a Protestant church in 1987.

Now we would like to have our marriage blessed by the Catholic Church. Does he have to have an annulment for this to happen? If so, where does he start?

The person who did not initiate an annulment case is called the *respondent* and must be informed that a case has begun. The respondent must be given an opportunity to offer testimony. That person, however, does not control the outcome of the case and is never asked to sign a form giving permission to remarry. I am sorry that someone gave you incorrect information on that subject.

A declaration of nullity decree is issued, usually by three judges, on the basis of documents and written testimony, with legal representation for both ex-spouses.

If the "respondent" refused to participate, that complicates but does not halt the process.

At www.AmericanCatholic.org, you can find our September 1998 article on this subject. Father John Catoir, J.C.D., answers four very common questions about annulments. Sister Victoria Vondenberger, R.S.M., J.C.L, head of the tribunal office for the Archdiocese of Cincinnati, wrote a sidebar entitled "What About the Rights of the Respondent?"

Annulment cases begin at the local parish. Someone on the parish staff collects the documents and testimony needed. Some dioceses have trained deacons, members of religious communities, or laypeople to help prepare tribunal cases.

Far from being a disagreeable, traumatizing re-living of the past, the annulment process has helped many people reach closure on a canonically invalid, non-sacramental marriage and prepare for a more Christ-centered second marriage.

What Is the Origin of the Celibacy Requirement for Priests?

When did the Roman Catholic Church begin requiring celibacy before a man could be ordained a priest? Why? Doesn't this suggest that marriage is inferior to celibacy?

Why doesn't the Roman Catholic Church allow a married clergy as the Eastern churches (Orthodox or Catholic) do?

By itself, a decision to remain single could mean very different things (great selfishness, great generosity, or inability to choose a spouse).

In Matthew 19:12, Jesus praises a celibacy practiced "for the sake of the kingdom." Optional, lifelong celibacy for men became more common among Egypt's desert hermits in the third century. In the year 303, the Council of Elvira (southern Spain) prohibited sexual intercourse between a married priest and his wife. By the mid-fourth century, marriage after ordination began to be prohibited.

There are various reasons—influence of cultic purity laws for Old Testament priests, concern to remove a possible conflict between loyalty to the church and to the interests of one's family, the teaching of Jesus cited above, and Saint Paul's teaching on celibacy (1 Corinthians 7:32–35).

Jesus cured the Apostle Peter's mother-in-law (Mark 1:30 and Luke 4:38). In Luke 18:28-30 and Matthew 19:27-30, Jesus speaks positively of a man who has chosen not to marry for the sake of the kingdom of God.

The Orthodox churches and Eastern Catholic churches ordain married men as priests but select their bishops from monks with a vow of celibacy. A married priest who becomes a widower may not remarry.

The Second Lateran Council (1139) declared clerical marriages invalid. In the last forty years, the Catholic church has allowed some married, Protestant ministers to be ordained Catholic priests after they became Catholics. Most of these priests are not in full-time parish ministry.

In his 1967 encyclical, *On Priestly Celibacy*, Pope Paul VI reaffirmed the Catholic church's requirement for priestly celibacy. Section 1579 of the *Catechism of the Catholic Church* says that "accepted with a joyous heart, celibacy radiantly proclaims the Reign of God."

A gospel-based celibacy does not devalue marriage; it is another way of serving the Lord. What matters most for both vowed celibates and married people is generous faithfulness.

How Can Episcopal Priests Become Roman Catholic Priests?

I know that some male Episcopalian priests have become Roman Catholics and been ordained as Catholic priests. Can they be assigned to parishes like regular Catholic priests? What about Episcopalian bishops and deacons?

Pope Leo XIII commissioned a study on this in 1895. The majority of its members concluded that ordinations in the Anglican church are null and void. The following year the pope wrote *Apostolicae Curae*, an apostolic letter confirming that position. Even so, some Catholics consider this an open question.

In 1966, Pope Paul VI gave a bishop's ring to Archbishop Michael Ramsey of Canterbury, an Anglican. In October of 2003, Pope John Paul II gave a pectoral cross to Archbishop Rowan Williams of Canterbury.

Several of Anglicanism's *39 Articles*, drafted in the sixteenth century, were carefully phrased to emphasize the differences in belief between the Church of England and the Roman Catholic church (for example, about transubstantiation).

Some Episcopalian priests have become Roman Catholics and later have been ordained as Roman Catholic priests. Cardinal John Henry Newman (died 1890) and Cardinal Henry Edward Manning (died 1892) did that. Manning was a widower when he became a Roman Catholic. Eventually, he became archbishop of Westminster, England.

Between 1982 and 2004, approximately a hundred and thirty married and twenty-five celibate Episcopal priests in the United States became Roman Catholics and were later ordained as Roman Catholic priests. (Although some Anglicans and Episcopalians describe themselves as "Catholics," in the rest of this response that term will be used to designate only "Roman Catholics.")

If Anglican bishops or priests and Protestant ministers are married when they became Catholic priests, they promise not to remarry should they become widowers. Those who were celibate at the time of ordination promise to remain celibate.

Roman Catholic men ordained as permanent deacons make a similar pledge, reflecting the practice of the Orthodox and Eastern Catholic churches. Episcopalian deacons who become Catholics and are ordained as Catholic deacons make the same promise.

Most married Roman Catholic priests serve as teachers, chaplains, or engage in some other non-parochial ministry.

Ecumenical relations between Roman Catholics and Episcopalians have been complicated by the decision of the United States Episcopal Church to ordain a priest in a same-sex union as a bishop and by the decision of several parts of the Anglican communion to ordain women priests and women bishops.

How Do Diocesan and Religious Priests Differ?

What is the difference between diocesan and religious priests?

Diocesan priests belong to a diocese or archdiocese; its bishop has the final say about their assignment, usually within the geographical boundaries of that diocese. Most diocesan priests work full-time in a parish. They can transfer permanently to another diocese only after several years of probation, allowing all concerned to evaluate the wisdom of such a move.

Religious priests belong to a religious community; their religious superior has the final say about their assignment. A religious priest is assigned to a parish only with the approval of the local bishop. Most religious priests minister outside a parish context. Rarely would a religious priest minister in the same diocese his entire life.

What Are the Requirements for Becoming a Deacon?

How are deacons chosen and trained in the Roman Catholic Church? What exactly can they do?

The roots for establishing the diaconate are described in Acts 6:1–7, which uses the verb *diakonein* ("to serve"). In Philippians 1:1, Saint Paul greets that church's overseers (*episcopoi*) and ministers (*diakonoi*). The office of *diakonos* is further described in 1 Timothy 3:8–13. Phoebe is called a *diakonos* (Romans 16:1).

Only over time did the church speak of bishop, priest, and deacon as levels within the sacrament of holy orders. The expectations for deacons are somewhat similar to the requirements for those being ordained a priest or a bishop. For example, the person feels a call to this vocation and the church must officially affirm that call. Although the man is ordained for a particular diocese or religious community, he must be ready to serve the entire church.

This requires adequate training in theology, liturgy, Scripture, canon law, preaching, and other areas. For those to be ordained permanent deacons, this training is usually done part-time over several years. In the case of married men preparing for the permanent diaconate, there are often training sessions for their wives. To my knowledge, no diocese will ordain a married man whose wife had not agreed to his being a deacon. Permanent deacons must be at least thirty-five years old.

A man who is not married when he is ordained a deacon must make a promise of celibacy for the rest of his life. If a married deacon becomes a widower, he can remarry if he receives a dispensation from the Holy See. This is granted on the basis of his bishop's recommendation, the great pastoral usefulness of the deacon's ministry and his having adequately provided for the care of any minor children.

For men ordained as "transitional" deacons (a step toward ordination to the priesthood), several years of previous full-time study are required.

Both permanent and transitional deacons must receive "faculties," permission to exercise this ministry from the bishop in the diocese where they serve. Their ordination does not of itself give them a right to exercise that ministry wherever and however they like. Priests and bishops also need faculties, from their local bishop or the bishop of Rome respectively.

Permanent deacons preach, baptize, witness marriages, and officiate at funeral services. The Rite of Ordination used for all deacons speaks of them as ministers of the Word of God, of the altar, and of charity. This last category includes service that is not predominantly sacramental (prison ministry, for example). In whatever way they serve, deacons build up the body of Christ.

Saint Stephen, one of the seven men chosen in Acts 6:5, was martyred about AD 36. He is considered the patron of deacons. Saint Lawrence, a deacon, was martyred around AD 258.

In Western Christianity by the year 1000, the office of deacon had pretty much become a step toward priestly ordination. There is, however, a contemporary reference to Saint Francis of Assisi, who died in 1226, as a deacon, though he is never described as a priest. Vatican II's *Lumen Gentium,* Dogmatic Constitution of the Church, envisioned the permanent diaconate (#29), which Pope Paul VI officially restored in the Latin church in 1967. The Orthodox churches had deacons continuously.

How Often Can Someone Receive the Anointing of the Sick?

How often can a person receive the sacrament of the anointing of the sick? One priest said four times in a calendar year was the limit.

According to the 1972 *Instruction for the Rite of Anointing of the Sick,* "Those who are seriously ill need the special help of God's grace in this time of anxiety, lest they be broken in spirit and, under the pressure of temptation, perhaps weakened in their faith" (#5).

Later it says: "Great care and concern should be taken to see that those of the faithful whose health is seriously impaired by sickness or old age receive this sacrament. A prudent or reasonably sure judgment, without scruple, is sufficient for deciding on the seriousness of an illness; if necessary a doctor may be consulted" (#8).

This sacrament can be repeated if the person has a relapse of the same illness (#9), if the person is about to undergo surgery for a serious illness (#10), or if elderly people "have become notably weakened even though no serious illness is present" (#11).

The church encourages us not to wait until someone is close to death before administering this sacrament. It probably would not be appropriate to give this anointing to someone about to have a medical test. The benefit of the doubt should ordinarily be given to someone requesting this sacrament if that person has been properly prepared for it.

CHAPTER FIVE

How We Pray

Is God Listening?

Several of my friends do not believe in God, Jesus Christ or the saints yet are lucky and have everything. Other friends and neighbors who do not go to church or donate to charity have the best of everything and are very lucky. I work hard, go to Sunday Mass, support the church and yet I don't get the best of everything and I am unlucky. My repeated prayers do not receive any answer. Why? Where is this loving God?

Yours is a common question, already asked centuries before Jesus was born. See Psalm 73 for one prayerful response to that question. It is not easy to see things as God sees them (see Matthew 16:23), but we must admit that God's ways can differ from our ways.

It sounds as though your basic needs are being met but you resent the extras that other people have. Perhaps their lives are not as stress-free as you suppose.

People who believe in God pray because they cannot live honestly without doing so. The first reason for praying is to praise God for being God. We can and should pray for what we need, but our prayers do not fill in gaps in God's knowledge or create a greater sense of urgency on God's part.

If believing in God guaranteed a rich and easy life, then why are there martyred saints or saints who died poor? Why did Job lose his children and his possessions? Why did Jesus die on a cross?

In our January 2005 issue, Father Michael Guinan, O.F.M., presented an overview of the honest and wide-ranging prayers in the book of Psalms. Our magazine's annual, variable column in 2005 was on the psalms, which are very candid prayers. Guinan's article and those twelve columns are available at www.AmericanCatholic.org.

Are Intercessory Prayers Worthwhile?

My husband and I recently got into a discussion about salvation and whether praying for a person's salvation makes any difference. He says that we cannot do anything for the salvation of another person. Is there any biblical evidence that we can?

Saint Paul wrote to the Christians in Thessalonika that he always prayed for them (2 Thessalonians 1:11). Earlier he had urged them to pray without ceasing (1 Thessalonians 5:17). James 5:16 urges us to pray for one another. The Gospels of Matthew and Luke especially devote a good deal of attention to Jesus' prayers and those of other people.

No amount of prayer for someone else can guarantee that he or she will respond generously to God's grace. We pray for others because we and they are part of the communion of saints, which involves three sets of people: those who are in heaven (who inspire us but do not need our prayers), plus those who are in purgatory (who need our prayers), as well as living people for whom we pray.

An honest relationship with God overflows into honest prayer. If you had a relative, friend, or coworker involved in some self-destructive behavior or relationship, wouldn't you pray that he or she wake up and realize where this is heading? Wouldn't your honest prayer eventually prompt you to say something or take some action to help that person?

Honest prayer is always about opening up to the grace of God. Your prayer for someone who is living does not guarantee that he or she will accept God's grace, but it makes you a better sign of God's grace for that individual. Perhaps that is precisely what God is counting on.

Is God Paying Attention?

In one of my mission magazines, I read about people of great faith, practicing their religion by loving and caring for their neighbors' physical and spiritual needs—yet thousands of these same people lack the barest necessities for a decent life—insufficient food (sometimes gathered from scrap heaps), no running water, poor sanitation, lack of healthcare. Regarding food and drink, the Bible says: "Your Father knows that you need them" (Luke 12:30) and "Seek first the Kingdom [of God] and his righteousness, and all these things shall be added unto you" (Matthew 6:33). Can you explain this discrepancy?

Yes, there is tremendous human need, very often among people who sincerely believe in God. Because the biblical passages that you cited are connected to prayer, let me start there.

We do not pray to call God's attention to things that we fear God may have overlooked or perhaps noticed yet forgot before taking appropriate action. We pray in order to acknowledge God and to recommit ourselves to live as people made in God's image. That includes recommitting ourselves to doing our part (however modest it may be) to ensure that the dignity of other people will be respected.

God's love and providence for us do not cancel out natural disasters (floods, hurricanes, and tornadoes, for example) or human sinfulness (such as murder, rape, or business fraud). Indeed, that same love prompts us to respond generously when others suffer, whether because of natural disasters or human sinfulness.

Our honest prayer leads us to do all that we can to promote God's justice for all men, women and children living today. We work hard at this, but we also know that however imperfect human justice is in this life, God's justice in the next life is total.

In Jesus' story about the rich man and Lazarus (see Luke 16:19–31), Jesus doesn't say whether either of them prayed. From the ending of the story, however, I presume that each of them did.

Jesus also does not say that the rich man was deliberately cruel toward Lazarus, whose needs may have been practically invisible to the

65

rich man. Radically honest prayer on the rich man's part would have challenged any idea that he and Lazarus had very different economic situations because God arranged things that way.

What Jesus *does* say in this story is that human judgment does not always reflect God's judgment. That is news to the rich man in this story, who even there presumes to command Abraham and Lazarus as he probably would have done had he met them in life.

Israel's pagan neighbors who believed in an afterlife assumed that their earthly economic and social positions would continue throughout eternity. They never considered that people's roles might be reversed, as the story in Luke's Gospel illustrates.

Blessed Mother Teresa of Calcutta knew the face of human suffering as well as anyone who has ever lived. What she saw did not amount to an indictment of God for failing to provide for people; it fueled her conviction that God does not intend for people to die from lack of proper food, housing, or medical care.

What Is "Ordinary Time"?

For much of the year, the weekday readings and prayers for Mass are indicated as "Ordinary Time." What does that term mean?

The Catholic Church's liturgical calendar starts with the Advent/Christmas season, includes a few weeks of Ordinary Time, then the Lent/Easter season, followed by Ordinary Time until the First Sunday of Advent, when a new liturgical year begins.

The 1969 "General Norms for the Liturgical Year and the Calendar" say that the Sundays in Ordinary Time "are devoted to the mystery of Christ in all its aspects" (#43).

Before the 1969 revision of the Roman Missal, most of these Sundays were known as the "Third Sunday after Pentecost." These Sundays became "Sundays in Ordinary Time" and actually start after the Baptism of the Lord until Ash Wednesday and then resume after Corpus Christi.

Although one of my friends refers to Ordinary Time as "boring time," I think this season is a valuable reminder that our lives include mostly ordinary events. But isn't that where we cooperate—or don't—with God's grace, where virtues become more normal or less so? Peak moments are wonderful, but no one can live in them forever.

In fact, peak moments require many ordinary moments. Couples do not reach a fiftieth wedding anniversary, for example, simply because of intense, key moments in their marriage. Their daily choices eventually create new peak moments in their lives. The same dynamic holds true for all married or single disciples of Jesus Christ. In the church's Ordinary Time, we journey closer to or away from Jesus.

What Is the Liturgy of the Hours?

My wife and I want to know more about the Liturgy of the Hours. Can you suggest resources to help us understand this form of prayer?

The Liturgy of the Hours (also called the Divine Office) was developed by monks as a way to sanctify the day and affirm that time ultimately belongs to God.

The Liturgy of the Hours was later adopted by diocesan priests, deacons, and members of other religious communities. After Vatican II, more laypeople took up the practice, praying the Hours privately or with a nearby religious community.

The two "hinges" of the Liturgy of the Hours are Morning Prayer (Lauds, prayed at daybreak or close to it) and Evening Prayer (Vespers, prayed at dusk or close to it). The other hours are Office of Readings, Midday Prayer, and Night Prayer.

Each day's cycle begins with the Office of Readings (Matins), a series of three psalms, then continues with a longer biblical reading and a passage from someone like Saint Jerome, Saint Augustine, or some other preacher, and closes with a prayer.

Shorter hours are prayed at mid-morning, midday, and mid-afternoon. The daily cycle concludes with Night Prayer, which is usually prayed after 6 PM.

The Bible's 150 psalms, together with Old Testament and New Testament canticles, are spread over a four-week cycle. These are complemented by other Scripture readings and short periods of silence.

Several publishers offer editions of the Liturgy of the Hours, which can be ordered from any Catholic bookstore. The books are often printed in four volumes, arranged seasonally.

The Liturgy of the Hours introduces people to the psalms, which reflect the full range of human emotions. Almost all of the one hundred and fifty psalms are prayed over a four-week cycle. The intercessions in the Liturgy of the Hours help people see themselves as part of a worldwide church.

Why Do Catholics Light Candles?

Can a non-Catholic go into a Catholic church and light a candle for someone? Why light candles?

A burning candle is like stretching out one's prayer. And for Christians, candle lighting is a reminder of Christ, the light of the world.

This custom has brought comfort to many people over the years. In September 2001, the nationally televised fundraiser responding to the September 11 attacks in Pennsylvania, New York City, and Washington, D.C., included many lighted candles on the New York and Los Angeles sets.

There is no special procedure to follow in church. Usually a sign indicates the monetary offering for the candle. Most people remain in prayer for a short time after they light a candle.

Why Do People Pray the Rosary?

Some of my Baptist friends have asked me questions about prayer. Matthew 6:7–8 says: "When you are praying, do not heap up empty phrases as the Gentiles do; for they think that they will be heard because of their many words. Do not be like them, for your Father knows what you need before you ask him." In light of this, why do Catholics pray the rosary? Why not keep the prayers short and direct? When I said that repetition can assist in meditation, they responded that meditation is not a Christian practice. They see it as a custom of non-Christian religions from the Middle East and the Far East.

Meditation is only for non-Christian religions founded in the Middle East or Far East? Not so! Saint Luke was clearly describing meditation when he wrote in his Gospel that Mary "kept all these things, reflecting on them in her heart" (2:19) and that Mary "kept all these things in her heart" (2:51).

Certainly your friends realize that Christianity itself began in the Near East. Meditation is not geographically based but is humanly based. Faith in Jesus requires moments of prayerful reflection, moments to ponder what God is doing when God's ways might seem very strange.

The length of prayers is not as important as the purity of intention. Even though the Canticle of Mary (Luke 1:46–55) is longer than the prayer of the Pharisee in the Temple (Luke 18:11–12), Mary's prayer is genuine because it is totally honest while the Pharisee's prayer is shorter but not totally honest.

The phrase "as the Gentiles do" may be the key to interpreting Matthew 6:7–8. The Gentile (pagan) prayer that Jesus condemns is an attempt to control God, a way of placing God in debt to the person who is praying.

The prayer that Jesus recommends does the reverse; it acknowledges an enormous debt toward God on the part of the praying person. Although this debt cannot be repaid, acknowledging it in prayer helps a person live honestly before God and in relation to all God's people. The longer Canticle of Mary reflected that honesty; the shorter prayer of the Pharisee in the Temple did not.

Immediately after the passage your friends cited, Jesus teaches the apostles to pray the Our Father. Is that prayer to be criticized for being too long?

Neither the Our Father nor the rosary seeks to give instructions to God. Both prayers arise from the same desire: To accept God's grace into one's life and cooperate generously with it.

Over the centuries, many Catholics have found the rosary an ideal prayer, partly because it reminds them of Mary's response to the Archangel Gabriel, "Here am I, the servant of the Lord: let it be with me according to your word" (Luke 1:38). That response became Mary's characteristic response to God throughout her life.

In the English section of www.vatican.va, if you search for "rosary," you can find Pope John Paul II's apostolic letter on the rosary (October 16, 2002. At www.AmericanCatholic.org you can find "The Rosary of the Virgin Mary," a condensed version of that letter, and other information about the rosary.

Meditation is for everyone. The fact that non-Christian religions encourage their own type of meditation does not make this a non-Christian form of prayer.

CHAPTER SIX

How We Grow Morally

Which Sin Is the Worst?

What is the worst sin that can be committed against Our Lord? What can we do to prevent such a sin?

A strong case can be made that the worst sin is religious hypocrisy—pretending that God loves all the things that I already like to do (usually very publicly) and that God despises all the people whom I despise. Jesus comes down very hard on this sin several times, especially in the story of the Pharisee and the tax collector praying in the Temple (Luke 18:9–14).

Other sins may do greater obvious damage (murder or adultery, for example), but religious hypocrisy insidiously suggests that God encourages immoral behavior, which is not true!

You asked about how we can avoid the worst sin. The answer is the same as for any sin: Open our hearts to God's grace and be willing to take the risks into which that grace may lead us (for example, forgiving someone).

Can a Religious Person Be a Hypocrite?

What is a religious hypocrite? I have always had a hard time understanding what a hypocrite is. Now some people are making it harder by adding the word religious.

A religious hypocrite is someone who creates God in his or her image—not the other way around as God intended. A religious hypocrite manipulates religion in order to look respectable or even heroic. This is the basis for Jesus' story of the Pharisee and the tax collector in the Temple (Luke 19:8–14).

A religious hypocrite likes worshipping a comfortable, non-threatening image of God rather than worshipping the totally honest and loving God of the Bible.

For example, a Christian racist is, by definition, a hypocrite because he or she is refusing to accept the Bible's affirmation that each person is made in God's image. Jesus and biblical prophets such as Amos, Micah, Isaiah, and Jeremiah gave very strong indictments of religious hypocrisy.

Does the Church Approve of Organ Donation?

How does the church view organ donation? My father passed away ten days ago and we donated his corneas. This question nags at me but what we did is a means of giving life to others who need help.

You wrote, "What we did is a means of giving life to others who need help...." I couldn't agree more. The *Catechism of the Catholic Church* says: "*Organ transplants* are in conformity with the moral law if the physical and psychological dangers and risks to the donor are proportionate to the good that is sought for the recipient. Organ donation after death is a noble and meritorious act and is to be encouraged as an expression of generous solidarity. [Organ transplants are] not morally acceptable if the donor or his proxy has not given explicit consent. Moreover, it is not morally admissible directly to bring about the disabling mutilation or death of a human being, even in order to delay the death of other persons" (#2296).

Some years ago an American couple donated the organs of their son murdered in a drive-by shooting in Italy. The church publicly applauded their generous decision that helped seven people.

To avoid potential conflict of interest, the medical team treating the dying patient should be separate from the team assisting a recipient.

The donation of your father's corneas was made with your consent before he died. There was no risk to the donor, who had already died. You have given the gift of sight to someone. The church blesses your action. Please be at peace with your generous, pro-life decision.

Is the Church Opposed to In Vitro Fertilization?

Is the Catholic Church against in vitro fertilization? If so, why? Isn't this a compassionate response for couples who want to have children but either or both spouses have medical conditions that make that unlikely?

The Catholic Church teaches that conception should occur within a wife's body, using an egg and the sperm from this husband and wife.

The Catholic Church considers immoral in vitro fertilization (IVF), the conception of a child in a Petri dish—even if the egg and sperm come from a married couple desiring to have a child (homologous artificial insemination and fertilization). Why? The unitive and procreative dimensions of marital intercourse have been separated through the introduction of technology that threatens the dignity of the human person. An added reason is that IVF procedures usually result in several zygotes, most of which are eventually discarded.

All the more does the Catholic Church consider it immoral if donated eggs and/or sperm are used (heterologous artificial insemination and fertilization). Surrogate motherhood, the use of a second woman to carry a child conceived in vitro (whether through homologous or heterologous procedures), is also considered immoral.

These situations are addressed in the *Catechism of the Catholic Church* (#2373–2379). On February 22, 1987, the Congregation for the Doctrine of the Faith issued *Donum Vitae*, Gift of Life, an instruction that addresses medically assisted human reproduction. That text is available through the Congregation's link at www.vatican.va.

The document *Dignitas Personae*, Dignity of the Person, prepared by the same congregation with the assistance of the Pontifical Academy for Life and dated September 8, 2008, addresses IVF, as well as genetic therapy and embryonic stem-cell research. Its full text can be found at the same website.

Our April 1997 article "Helping Childless Couples Conceive," which explains the morality of several techniques used to assist conception, is available at www.AmericanCatholic.org.

Is in vitro fertilization a compassionate response to couples who want to have children but one or both spouses have medical conditions that make that unlikely? Not really. The *Catechism of the Catholic Church* notes: "A child is not something *owed* to one, but is a *gift*. The 'supreme gift of marriage' is a human person. A child may not be considered a piece of property, an idea to which an alleged 'right to a child' would lead. In this area, only the child possesses genuine rights: the right 'to be the fruit of a specific act of the conjugal love of parents,' and 'the right to be respected as a person from the moment of conception'" (#2378, quoting *Donum Vitae*, II, 8).

The *Catechism* concludes its treatment of in vitro fertilization with these words: "The Gospel shows that physical sterility is not an absolute evil. Spouses who still suffer from infertility after exhausting legitimate medical procedures should unite themselves with the Lord's Cross, the source of all spiritual fecundity. They can give expression of their generosity by adopting abandoned children or performing demanding services for others" (#2379).

Must I Boycott Businesses That Support Causes I Reject?

A boycott has been urged for companies that support Planned Parenthood. The grocery store where I shop, part of a chain, is on that list. I am a widow on Social Security and have big medical bills. My nest egg is dwindling rapidly. This store is the cheapest in the area and has what I need. Under these circumstances, am I obliged to boycott this store?

The moral issue here is described as "cooperation in evil." Are you promoting artificial contraception or abortion if you continue to shop at that grocery store? The fact that you raise this question indicates that you want to act in a morally good way.

Moral theologians speak of "formal cooperation" (direct) and "material cooperation" (indirect). Formal cooperation means making someone else's immoral action one's own, willfully joining in it. Material cooperation indirectly contributes to another person's immoral action without truly assenting to it.

If an abortion is performed in a hospital, those who willfully assist a doctor in performing it are involved in formal cooperation with evil. A lab technician in the same hospital could be involved in material cooperation if he or she unwillingly participates.

People who manufactured Zyklon-B gas, used to murder Jews and others at Nazi concentration camps, were involved in formal cooperation with evil if they knew how that gas was being used. People who bought other products from the company that manufactured Zyklon-B gas were involved in material cooperation—unless they chose that company precisely because it made the gas used to murder people. In that case, theirs was formal cooperation in evil.

A person's moral responsibility is proportionate to how direct the connection is to the immoral action, how much the person knows about that connection and what other options are available to this person.

In our increasingly interconnected world, it has become very difficult to avoid all material cooperation in evil. The drug company that has a patent on a life-saving medicine that I need may also make drugs intended to cause a spontaneous abortion.

Some people even buy stock in companies that they do not support—in order to have the right to initiate a stockholders' resolution about some product or procedure to which they have a moral objection.

Must you boycott this grocery store chain? Not every call for a boycott creates a moral obligation to join it. That is a prudential judgment about which conscientious people may disagree.

On the other hand, no decision is simply economic—without moral implications. Some boycotts have resulted in more just compensation for workers or greater protection for their rights and safety.

The Interfaith Center on Corporate Responsibility can be a valuable resource in these matters. Their website is www.iccr.org.

If at some future date you can do your grocery shopping at another store without great hardship to yourself, I encourage you to do so—as long as there are valid reasons for a boycott. For the present, however, I cannot say that it is sinful for you to shop at that chain store.

Must I Vote for the Pro-life Candidate?

What is the moral responsibility of a Catholic about voting? Let's assume one candidate's voting records shows that he or she supports abortion. Let's assume the other candidate is definitely pro-life and a very conservative individual. Is it sinful for a Catholic to vote for a candidate who supports abortion because the voter feels that supporting one party is crucial? If so, what kind of sin is this?

Catholic moral teaching says that Catholic voters should consider a wide range of issues when deciding for whom to vote. In their 1999 document Faithful Responsibility, a statement to and for Catholics regarding political responsibility, the United States Catholic bishops wrote: "Our moral framework does not easily fit the categories of right or left, Democrat or Republican. Our responsibility is to measure every party and platform by how its agenda touches human life and dignity."

Later in the same document they stated: "As bishops, we do not seek the formation of a religious voting block, nor do we wish to instruct persons on how they should vote by endorsing or opposing candidates. We hope that voters will examine the position of candidates on the full range of issues, as well as on their personal integrity, philosophy and performance.

"We are convinced that a consistent ethic of life should be the moral framework from which to address all issues in the political arena. We urge our fellow citizens to see beyond party politics, to analyze campaign rhetoric critically, and to choose their political leaders according to principle, not simply party affiliation or mere self-interest."

They also wrote: "We believe that every human life is sacred from conception to natural death; that people are more important than things; and that the measure of every institution is whether or not it enhances the life and dignity of the human person."

What Does the Church Teach About Stem-cell Research?

What is the difference between research on stem cells from animals, adult humans, and embryos? Are all of these sins? Does the Bible address this issue?

Research on animals sometimes identifies treatments that can be adapted for humans. Animal research needs to be conducted scientifically and ethically.

Stem cells from adult humans (and this includes stem cells obtained from umbilical cords) have been effective for some conditions. The editorial in our May 2007 issue (see www.AmericanCatholic.org) explains the issues involved.

The Catholic Church has opposed research that uses embryonic stem cells because this is human life created simply to obtain such stem cells, a human life that is inevitably destroyed in this process. This is unethical because it suggests that human life at that stage can be ended for the sake of research.

Thomas Shannon's *Catholic Update*, "Stem-cell Research: How Catholics Ethnics Guide Us," is available at the website cited above.

In November 2007, Catholic News Service reported that the journals *Cell* and *Science* had published articles about two studies showing that human skin cells can be preprogrammed to work as effectively as embryonic stem cells in reproducing any of the 220 types of cells in the human body.

These studies were conducted by Shinya Yamanaka of Kyoto University (Japan) and by Junying Yu and James Thomson of the University of Wisconsin-Madison.

The National Catholic Bioethics Center (www.ncbcenter.org) in Philadelphia said of these studies, "The methods outlined in these papers fully conform to what we have hoped to see for some time. Such strategies should continue to be pursued and strongly promoted, as they should help to steer the entire field of stem-cell research in a more explicitly ethical direction by circumventing the moral quagmire associated with destroying human embryos."

Are "Do Not Resuscitate" Orders Moral?

My mother, an eighty-one-year-old devout Catholic, lives in a nursing home. It has asked my brother, who has her medical power of attorney, to sign a Do Not Resuscitate (DNR) form for her. What is the Catholic Church's teaching on DNR forms?

Does this nursing home require a DNR form for all its patients? If so and if she is capable of consenting, she could sign the form herself. A medical power of attorney form indicates the patient's wishes about specified procedures, including a DNR order. If the person is incapable of making these decisions, then the designated person does so.

If your mother did not consent, would this nursing home evict her? Does any nursing home require a signed DNR order as a condition for residency there? A lawyer could point out relevant state laws on this matter.

If this is genuinely informed consent, signing a DNR form for oneself or for another is not inherently immoral because it identifies the extent of medical care that a person wishes to receive.

Life is a gift from God, to be welcomed, nurtured, and cherished. There is, however, no moral obligation to prolong it by every means possible. Some medical procedures are morally optional. All life comes from God and must eventually be returned to God.

In their book *Life Issues, Medical Choices: Questions and Answers for Catholics* (Servant), Janet Smith and Christopher Kaczor address the question, "What is the difference between ordinary means and extraordinary means of preserving life?"

Smith and Kaczor describe ordinary means as "treatments that are more beneficial than burdensome to the patient and others" and extraordinary means as "treatments in which the benefits do not correspond to the burdens of treatment." They go on to write: "In determining whether or not a given procedure should be begun or continued, patients and physicians must assess the likely benefits and burdens of the procedure for a particular patient...what is in question is whether the *procedure* is worthwhile, not whether the *person's life* is worthwhile."

How Can I Balance My Moral and Professional Obligations?

As an ophthalmologist, I have several patients who do not have legal driving vision because of decreased central vision or constriction of their side vision. Although I point out to these patients that their vision does not meet legal driving standards, many of them continue to drive. The state where I live does license examinations every five years.

Because of the doctor-patient relationship, I am not inclined to report them to the state authorities. On the other hand, if I do not do so, am I seriously sinning by failing to protect other people from these drivers? Have I met my moral obligation by simply reminding them that they do not meet legal standards?

You clearly have a well-developed conscience, including a readiness to ask how your professional responsibilities relate to the common good of society.

A moral theologian whom I consulted offered this advice: Try to be a bit more persuasive with these patients, helping them to realize that they are endangering the common good of society—including their own family members.

How would these patients feel if one of their grandchildren was injured by someone with eyesight as bad as theirs? Calm but persistent reasoning on your part may convince some patients to discontinue driving.

This approach, however, may not work in all cases. Have you discussed this situation in generic terms with nearby ophthalmologists or with your state licensing board?

Although a patient's right to confidentiality is very important, it is not absolute. A doctor who fears that a patient is suicidal, for example, may be justified in breaking that confidentiality in order to seek additional assistance.

Someone could argue that, having tried and failed to dissuade these patients from driving, your decision to report such visual impairment is a form of self-defense. In fact, you could be killed or injured by a driver who does not meet your state's vision requirements.

When I consulted a friend who is a lawyer, he responded, "The general theory of civil law is that 'experts' are not responsible for the freely chosen actions of 'competent' others (thus the suicide or irrational danger to others exceptions) once they have clearly informed them of the dangers which their actions present to themselves or others."

At one level, you have met your moral obligation by informing these patients that they do not meet legal standards. But having done so, this issue continues to trouble your conscience. Perhaps that indicates your conscience is experiencing a new phase, a "growth spurt" on this issue.

Did Pornography Ruin His Life?

My daughter's oldest son is fifteen and a half. When he was thirteen, she discovered that he had viewed pornography on the computer. She admits that she wasn't vigilant enough about his computer activity, but now she watches it carefully.

Recently, however, someone told her that her son's life is ruined because he viewed pornography at a young age—and that nothing can change this. My daughter is sick with guilt and asked me what she should do. I do not know if anything can be done to right this wrong. What can I say to give her some encouragement?

No, your grandson's life is not ruined by the viewing you described. Nothing can be done now to erase that past, distressing as it is. With help from your daughter and others, your grandson can learn to recognize that pornography implicitly denies that human sexuality is a profound gift from God. The Bible teaches us that we must always recognize people as our brothers and sisters loved by God—never as mere objects for our pleasure.

On the other hand, habitually viewing pornography and accepting these images as normal corrupts a person's understanding of sexuality. Pornography has become an addiction for more and more people who prefer virtual relationships that require no self-sacrifice over genuine relationships. Those always involve self-sacrifice.

It is true that people frequently need help processing and interpreting many types of experience. Sometimes professional assistance is needed, depending on the gravity of the event, its duration, and other factors.

I continue to be amazed by the number of people who are quick to say that a particular incident inevitably ruins a person's life. That sounds almost blasphemous because only God could know such a thing. An individual's future unfolds according to the choices that he or she makes. It seems to me that those who say, "It's all over now," have missed what Jesus teaches about repentance, conversion, and new life.

God alone is absolute. Unfortunately, human beings sometimes act as though they can become absolute simply by speaking about God. Not so.

Your daughter is, I hope, doing more than closely monitoring her son's computer activity. Has she challenged the warped view of life that pornographic images present? Why should furtive viewing of pornography be considered more realistic than an open, genuinely loving relationship with someone?

An example from my years of teaching high school religion may help here. I once suggested to my sophomore students that life is like a VCR tape (remember those?) that moves only forward. Whatever we have done or failed to do—that part of a person's life—cannot be rewound and taped over with new and better material, totally erasing the original decisions from memory. The same is true for material on a DVD.

We can, however, decide which things will go on our life's tape (or DVD) in the future. We can and must dilute the evil that have already committed while reinforcing the good things we have done.

We do this diluting and reinforcing by means of our future choices, not by dwelling on past mistakes. We need to acknowledge our mistakes, confess our sins, and then make the daily choices that cumulatively will indicate which of our past choices represent "the real me."

The document *Pornography and Violence in the Communications Media: A Pastoral Response* (Pontifical Council for Social Communications, 1989) states: "Even so called 'soft-core' pornography can have a progressively desensitizing effect, gradually rendering individuals morally numb and personally insensitive to the rights and dignity of others.

"Exposure to pornography can also be—like exposure to narcotics—habit-forming and can lead individuals to seek increasingly 'hard-core' and perverse material. The likelihood of anti-social behavior can grow as this process continues." The entire document can be accessed through www.vatican.va.

In time, all of us become what we choose, that is, what we accept as normal, ordinary and "no big deal." God allows more U-turns than the person who told your daughter that her son's life was ruined.

What Financial Obligations and Rights Do Bishops Have?

Is there a limit to the amount of money that a bishop who heads a diocese can spend? Does he need anyone's permission? If so, whose? Also, can a bishop seize property belonging to a parish or religious community?

Before a local United States bishop can spend more than $500,000 (or one million dollars if the diocese has more than 500,000 Catholics), he must obtain the permission of his diocesan finance council, the college of consultors and any interested parties, as explained in Canon 1292, #1. Adjustments for inflation are noted at www.usccb.org/norms/1292.1-htm.

Even with such permission, United States bishops must currently obtain the Holy See's permission for any debt (building or buying, selling or exchanging property) exceeding five million dollars or (ten million dollars for a diocese with more than 500,000 Catholics). These amounts were established by a decree from the Congregation for Bishops on March 31, 2004.

According to Canon 1276, #1, the head of a diocese, archdiocese, or religious community is "to exercise careful vigilance over the administration of all the goods which belong to public juridic persons subject to him...."

A parish's financial accounts and its immovable property make up part of the patrimony for which a bishop has responsibility.

The basic unit of the Catholic Church is the diocese—not the parish. A bishop, however, holds parish property in trust. Each diocese establishes how much money a parish can spend on its own authority and for what amount of money the parish must obtain the bishop's permission.

The Western church's Code of Canon Law establishes the general framework of rights and obligations within the church. Canons 1254 through 1310 address ownership issues. The Code of Law for the Eastern churches spells out the procedures followed by those churches.

Parish property is sometimes separately incorporated or may be part of the "corporation sole" of the diocese where it is located.

A religious community could present a property dispute to the Congregation for Institutes of Consecrated Life and Societies of Apostolic Life. If its decision went against the local bishop, he could appeal it to the Apostolic Signatura, the Catholic Church's highest court.

A group of parishioners could present a property dispute with their local bishop to the Congregation for Clergy. An appeal to the Signatura might be possible.

CHAPTER SEVEN

How We Grow in Faith and Practice It

Can Questions Help Faith Grow?

I have been intermittently going to the Catholic Church for approximately fif-
teen years. My wife, a lifelong Catholic, and I have been married for three
years. I am now a catechumen in the RCIA (Rite of Christian Initiation of
Adults) program.

I still question my faith a great deal. I know that Saint Anselm said some-
thing about faith and questioning. Does my questioning certain things prevent
me from becoming a Catholic?

Questions do not destroy faith; indifference destroys faith. God is not
fragile and can withstand any questions that we ask. We, however, are
not always ready to deal with God's response as it comes to us from
Scriptures and through the life of the faith community. Saint Anselm of
Canterbury (died 1109) famously described theology as "faith seeking
understanding." Questions are part of the understanding process.

Perhaps you should identify your most serious questions about the
Catholic Church. If you cannot accept the real presence of Jesus in the
Eucharist, you are not ready to be baptized. If you question whether vio-
let vestments should be worn on the Sundays of Lent, you can be baptized as you seek to understand this practice.

How Can I Have a Childlike Faith?

I have observed that all adults have had things happen to them that can cause
them to lose faith. People then build up a psychological wall to prevent that

from happening again. The Bible, however, speaks of having a childlike faith. As a fifty-four-year-old adult, I would like to know: How can I get back my childlike faith? If one loses faith, how can a childlike faith be recovered?

All adult believers must find a satisfactory answer to your question if they are to continue on their faith journey. Otherwise, they merely remember faith as a pleasant but irrecoverable childhood feeling.

When you were a child, when you made your First Communion, did you have the same faith that your parents or grandparents had? In one way, yes, but in another way, no.

Faith exists primarily in living persons, in women, men, and children who have unique faith journeys. In that sense, you and your parents or grandparents could not have exactly the same faith because you did not have identical life experiences.

You had the same faith in the sense that you believed in the same God. But you could not believe in exactly the same way because your life experiences were so different. An elderly person who has nurtured a lifelong faith in Jesus has, in fact, previously had a childhood faith, a teen faith, a young adult faith, and a middle-aged faith.

When people speak as though they had real faith when they were children but lost it while growing up, what they are calling "lost" faith could, in fact, be a stunted faith, one frozen in time because they are not incorporating into it their good and bad life experiences.

The faith of a seven-year-old is fine for a seven-year-old, but it cannot support the more serious questions of a fifty-four-year-old. Whoever idealizes his or her childhood faith cannot grow in a faith that develops by pondering and praying over one's life experiences, aided by Scripture, prayer, the sacraments, and the help of fellow believers.

The Gospel of Luke says that Mary, the mother of Jesus, "treasured all these words and pondered them in her heart" (2:19). Indeed, that describes everyone who grows in faith.

The Gospel of Matthew tells us that when the disciples asked who is the greatest in the kingdom of heaven, Jesus "Truly I tell you, unless you change and become like children, you will never enter the kingdom of heaven" (18:3).

Writing about this passage in the *New Jerome Biblical Commentary*, Benedict Viviano, O.P., explains that the child here "serves as a symbol for humility, not because children are naturally humble, but because they are dependent." Viviano goes on to point out that *turn* "is a Semitism [Hebrew expression] for change, conversion."

Jesus was emphasizing the honesty of children in realizing that they are dependent. Growing older can reinforce the illusion that we no longer depend on anyone. In that case, our childhood faith is bound to become "lost." On the other hand, growing older can help us to see God at work—as Mary did—even when life is difficult.

How Can Blended Families Promote Faith?

My husband and I are now married in the Catholic Church. Our previous marriages were not Catholic marriages. Between the two of us, we have three daughters.

After his divorce, my husband returned to the Catholic Church. He regrets not introducing religion to his daughters, who are now nineteen and twenty-four. They live with us but do not understand or want to know about the "Catholic Dad" they suddenly have. Because of their questions and disagreements with the Catholic Church's teachings, my twelve-year-old daughter is now questioning the upbringing that I have been teaching and living as I promised to do when she was baptized in the Catholic Church. This is perhaps our biggest challenge as a blended family. Any advice or suggestions would be appreciated.

I think it is important to begin by saying that the one-size-fits-all approach does not fully respect how a person grows in faith. True, the object of our faith (God) does not change, but our ability to understand and appreciate God develops. Faith has content (truths about God and revelation) but faith is also a relationship, which must either grow or decline.

Different issues become urgent at various points in a person's life. What someone learns about God at age five is true as far as it goes, but by itself it probably cannot fully support that person's faith at age twelve, nineteen, twenty-four, or sixty-seven.

The best approach may be for your husband to explain to his daughters why, in recent years, faith in general and being a Catholic in particular have become so important to him—what was lacking before and how his life is different because of this change.

This may be difficult for him to do without seeming to run down their mother. He probably needs to speak about his own blindness regarding faith when the daughters were growing up. You may be able to help him prepare for this talk. If their birth mother is in their lives, he should probably encourage them to ask her to explain how she came to whatever faith she now has.

Your twelve-year-old daughter has her own challenges to faith. She is certainly influenced by her stepsisters, but the situation is not likely to improve until she more fully owns her faith issues and begins facing them seriously. Her stepsisters' questions and disagreements are exactly that—*their* questions and disagreements.

If you talk to other Catholic mothers who now have or recently have had twelve-year-old daughters but are not in blended families, you will probably hear some of the same doubts and objections that your twelve-year-old daughter is voicing. Her situation has been influenced by her stepsisters but was not completely created by them.

You can help your daughter in her faith growth, but you cannot do that work for her. You might want to begin by acknowledging that some faith matters that seemed very clear to you at age eight, for example, became much less clear at age twelve—and how you dealt with that.

Your goal is not to give her the total faith that sustains you today but to help her believe that her faith issues are not insurmountable. In some ways, doubt can be an invitation to deeper faith. Perhaps that is what the father of a boy from whom Jesus expelled a demon understood when the father said to Jesus, "I do believe, help my unbelief" (Mark 9:24).

Your daughter is quietly but regularly observing how deeply faith is influencing your life. You are probably giving her a better example than you suspect. Being ready to speak about your own faith journey in a way appropriate for her age is probably the greatest help that you can offer her now.

Does God Determine My Actions?

If God knows all things, then God knows what I will do next, including the sins I may commit. If God has a plan for us, how can we have free will?

This issue has been a topic of discussion among Christians for centuries. Human beings are limited by time; we necessarily think in terms of past, present, and future. The problem you raise, however, comes from imposing those limitations on God—for whom past, present, and future are equally present.

If your approach is correct, wouldn't God be equally responsible for the compassion of Florence Nightingale and the abomination caused by the 9/11 terrorists? Doesn't such reasoning turn good and evil into personal preferences (for example, I like coin collecting but you like stamp collecting)? More importantly, doesn't it make God indifferent to both?

That cannot be. God very much prefers good (the proper use of human freedom) over evil (the distorted use of human freedom). "The woman whom you gave to be with me, she gave me fruit from the tree, and I ate," a guilty Adam explained to God (Genesis 3:12). Eve then blamed the serpent, which had accomplished its mission.

Adam and Eve misused their freedom and in talking with God, in fact, denied that they were ever free. May God help us to avoid that mistake!

Was It God's Will?

Does God have a direct hand in a person's death? Or does randomness play into one's death and only then does God's judgment determine a person's fate? If two people are involved in an accident—plane crash, car crash, tornado, whatever—and one of them dies, does that mean the person who died was less important in God's eyes?

In an extremely wide sense, whatever happens is God's will because God created everything. The huge problem with saying that, however, is that contradictory things appear to be God's will. We know, however, that God has a clear preference between good and evil.

Adolf Hitler's death camps killed approximately six million Jews and four million gentiles. Was that God's will? No. The Allies defeated Hitler's war machine and closed the concentration camps. Was that God's will? Yes.

We need to be very careful about using the expression "God's will." Doesn't our experience show that people most often use this term to describe someone *else's* suffering? They do this, it appears, to restore some kind of order in a seemingly chaotic world.

In the book of Job, three friends think that his suffering reveals God's will. At the book's conclusion, God denies that explanation. In the Gospel of John, Jesus' disciples assume that the man born blind was being punished for his sins or those of his parents. Jesus rejects both interpretations of the man's blindness (9:3).

I once saw a three-panel cartoon. In the first panel, God is standing on a cloud, looking pensive. In the next panel, God goes to a wire container with numbered balls (like those used in bingo) and picks one out. In the final panel, a man walks down a street and masonry from a balcony comes loose and is about to fall on him.

I do not think that tragedies happen that way—and I doubt that cartoonist did either. Some human suffering is created by people (I smoke three packs of cigarettes a day and then develop emphysema or I drive too fast on a slippery, winding road and have an accident). Other suffering is created by forces of nature (people die in hurricanes, volcanic eruptions, earthquakes, floods, fires). Many more problems, however, are caused by the misuse of human freedom than by what insurance policies call "acts of God."

God's will is that each person live as someone made in God's image and likeness. God's will is that we share eternal life with God. Must God do anything and everything to guarantee this? No, because that would render human freedom meaningless.

In the First Letter to the Thessalonians, Saint Paul writes, "For this is the will of God, your sanctification;..." (4:3). God's overall will for us is certain; how we respond is not so clear. We dare not exalt human freedom to the detriment of God, who created it. We likewise should not use "God's will" as a way of undercutting human freedom and the importance of our daily decisions.

In Jesus' parable about the Last Judgment (Matthew 25:31–46), we can easily imagine that those who were saved and those who were condemned had very different ideas about God's will—especially when it came to feeding the hungry, clothing the naked, and the other works of mercy that Jesus lists.

If those types of suffering are God's will, then why bother to try to alleviate them? Jesus, however, praises those who respond with compassion to the needs of their brothers and sisters. He condemns those who deny compassion to those in need. Perhaps those who were condemned thought that it was God's will that hungry people are hungry. Such an idea would certainly justify refusing to help anyone.

It's too easy to say that all suffering which happens to other people is God's will. If that were true, then every work of compassion would oppose God's will. The Scriptures deny that.

One person's death and another's survival in an accident—neither has anything to do with their respective importance in God's eyes. Ultimately, we have to admit that God and God's ways of dealing with people are great mysteries. Using reason enlightened by faith, we can rightly probe these mysteries, but eventually we must admit with Job that we cannot question God as equals.

Is God Both Good and Evil?

My friend says that God is both good and evil because God is all-encompassing. I say God is only good. How can I defend my position?

Your question has been discussed by people over the centuries. If God is both good and evil, isn't God divided, with parts competing against each other? Is that the God of the Bible?

The second creation story in the book of Genesis (2:4b–25) affirms that the entire world as created by God is good and that evil entered the world by the misuse of human freedom.

In the ancient world, dualism, the belief that the world is composed of two equally powerful and warring elements, was very common. It seemed the best way to explain life's constant mixture of light and darkness. The biblical writers see things quite differently. According to them, evil was not created directly by God; its possibility, however, flows from God's creation. If you eliminate that possibility, you take away the freedom necessary for love, service, and forgiveness.

If God is both good and evil, doesn't that eventually blame God for every evil that I do? Isn't that starting with original sin (our wounded human condition) and then projecting it back onto God, creating God in *my* image instead of the other way around?

Doesn't your friend's solution to the problem of evil create an even bigger problem? Doesn't it raise a much more serious question: Why trust a God who is only partially good? Both Judaism and Christianity suggest that your friend's solution, in fact, does not work. Some answers are more simple than true.

Does the Devil Cause Evil?

Does the devil inflict evil upon people to test or tempt them? If so, does that make the devil as powerful as God? As a fallen angel, the devil must have some power. Does the devil cause bad things to happen to one person and not to another?

The devil is a fallen angel, a creature. No creature can be more power-ful than God. That is the enticement that the serpent gave to Eve and gives to everyone else, but it always falls flat.

The Christian tradition has often called the devil "the father of lies." The devil's power comes from people ready to believe his claims, ready to accept his supposed shortcuts, which are, in fact, always dead ends. For this reason the Easter Vigil liturgy invites people to renounce "the glamour of evil." That liturgy also asks, "Do you reject sin, so as to live in the freedom of God's children?" When people live according to the devil's standards, they are not more free even though temptations sug-gest they will be.

Most of the evil that people experience comes from their own or someone else's abuse of human freedom. The book of Genesis is very insistent on this point. The devil's power comes mostly from people ready to believe the devil's lies—as Adam, Eve, and their descendants have. Genuine diabolical possession is possible.

Although we cannot afford to ignore the devil, neither can we abdi-cate our God-given, human freedom. We cannot collapse all evil into the work of supernatural forces beyond our control. Jesus has con-quered the devil for us. Our lives should affirm that victory.

How Can I Feel Close to God?

I am a fifty-three-year-old wife, mother, and grandmother. Lately, I am hav-ing a difficult time praying and concentrating. I do not feel very close to God, who has been there so many times for me in a way that I could feel. I have dealt with depression most of my life and now cannot do the walking that helped me combat the depression.

Even though I try to pray the rosary each day on my way to work, some-times I realize that my mind is so far away that I wonder what I'm saying. What can I do to get my faith back and feel close to God as I used to? Right now I feel much more turmoil than peace.

Sometimes a person's faith journey may seem stalled or at a standstill. That may be your situation now. In order for their spiritual journeys to continue, people may need to identify and deal with whatever obstacles they are experiencing. For example, someone might say, "I am a good person. I try to do my best for God, my family and for others, and yet I still have to deal with many unfair and unjust things." Such a feeling is very real and will continue to hamper that person's faith journey until the situation is addressed adequately in prayer.

Perhaps you describe your present obstacle differently. Whatever it is, I encourage you to deal with it through prayer, reading, journaling, and/or conversation with a believer whom you respect.

Perhaps you are angry with God but are reluctant to admit this because that may sound as though you are ungrateful. Saying "I shouldn't feel this way" will always be an obstacle to cooperating with God's grace. In fact, we should not act on all our feelings, but we are certainly headed for trouble whenever we deny their very existence and our freedom to reinterpret those feelings.

God is not fragile and can take a little heat if you need to vent. If you read the Bible carefully, some of the most sincere prayers (for example, Jeremiah 20:7–18 and many of the Psalms) could not have felt very consoling at the time they were uttered. That did not make them any less worthwhile as prayers.

Although consolation in prayer is fine whenever we experience it, the real purpose of prayer is opening oneself to God's grace and cooperating with it.

How Can I Avoid Being Hurt?

I have been in abusive relationships for much of my life. I seem to pick the same type of partners and am constantly being hurt. What can I do differently?

You were created in God's image and likeness. Saying, "I deserve better than the kinds of relationships I have had" may be the best start you

ANSWERS TO CATHOLIC QUESTIONS

can make. If you respect yourself, other people will also.

Your diocesan Catholic Charities or a local mental health agency can help you contact a professional counselor with whom you can discuss this situation.

How Can I Explain My Faith?

My two closest friends have a big problem with the fact that I am Catholic. One believes there is no God but only a higher power affecting our minds and what we do. The other says that I am always worrying about whether something is moral while he says he can become a better person from experiencing drugs, alcohol, and smoking. We often argue over things like this because I try to explain how God and my Catholic faith have affected my life. I don't try to get them to become Catholic but I wonder how I should handle their attempts to turn me away from Catholicism.

Not believing that God exists is really too simple because you would have to go through an infinite number of mental images of God, rejecting them one by one. If an atheist rejects one image of God, a believer can truthfully say, "In fact, that's not the God in whom I believe."

Atheists try to save time by rejecting *all* possible images of God. That proves, however, only that no single mental image captures God completely. Any believer could have told them that already. A bumper sticker from the 1960s may apply here: "My God is not dead. Sorry about yours."

Perhaps these two friends are probing to see how deep your faith goes, whether it can withstand their pressure. Following Jesus will always have a steep price of some type—but one that is worth paying.

What Is the Spiritual Role of Fathers?

What does the Catholic Church teach about the role of fathers in the family? This seems to be a neglected area today.

The Rite of Baptism for Children may say it best. After the priest or deacon blesses the mother, he blesses the father, saying: "God is the giver of all life, human and divine. May he bless the father of this child. He and his wife will be the first teachers of their child in the ways of faith. May they be also the best of teachers, bearing witness to the faith by what they say and do, in Christ Jesus our Lord. Amen."

All fathers have a natural duty to protect, provide for, and educate their daughters and sons while being loving and supportive husbands. Catholic fathers have an added responsibility to be role models of faith and of virtue as companions on the faith journeys of their children. That instructor/companion role, which is influenced by their family and cultural upbringing, changes as children age but never disappears.

The Bible offers many teachings, especially in the wisdom literature of the Hebrew Scriptures, about the role of fathers. The New Testament letters address this responsibility, especially in 1 Thessalonians 2:11–12, Ephesians 6:4, Colossians 3:21, and 1 John 2:13–14. Everything that Jesus says about being a disciple applies to dads.

The *Catechism of the Catholic Church* addresses the duties of parents in sections 2221–2231. The text advises parents to regard their sons and daughters as children of God and to respect them as human persons (#2222).

In recent years, both single and married Catholic men have begun participating in men's prayer groups, Scripture study, and retreats on male spirituality. The National Resource Center for Catholic Men can be contacted at www.nrccm.org.

CHAPTER EIGHT

How We Experience Forgiveness and Redemption

When Should I Forgive?

When is it appropriate to forgive someone? What does forgiving someone really mean? Is forgiveness the same as reconciliation?

Who benefits most from forgiveness—the one being forgiven or the person doing the forgiving? If you see forgiveness as a gift to people being forgiven, you will probably wait until they seek forgiveness or clearly indicate an openness to it. If you see forgiveness primarily as a gift to yourself, you will probably forgive more quickly, and know that they may never recognize their need to seek forgiveness.

In Jesus' parable of the Prodigal Son (Luke 15:11–32), when did the father decide to forgive the younger son? When the son begged forgiveness? Or long before? Wasn't the father looking down the road for that son because the father had *already* decided to forgive him?

If the younger son had never "come to his senses" (v. 17), would the father have been foolish to have forgiven him? Not at all. Once the father turned the case over to God, he would have been free of resentment, even though he would not have experienced the consolation of his son's repentance.

There is a unique freedom experienced by the person who decides to forgive. That is true regardless of whether the other party ever realizes any need to seek forgiveness.

A firm, long-term refusal to forgive is a decision to put one's life "on hold" until the other person asks for forgiveness. Being put on hold happens with telephone conversations, but why do it to yourself voluntarily?

Unfortunately, people sometimes think that forgiveness requires lying to themselves—that the offensive action or omission never happened, that it didn't really do much damage. That approach to forgiveness can keep a person in an abusive situation, lead to serious financial loss, or put someone's life in jeopardy. It's not forgiveness to make excuses for another person's addiction or its negative consequences. People sometimes talk, however, as if forgiveness is the same as codependency: pretending that someone else's self-destructive behavior is OK. In that mistaken approach, forgiveness must be withheld to avoid codependency.

Additionally, the person who needs to ask forgiveness can mistakenly think that, once it is received, everything is restored. Not exactly. If I put a baseball through your window, I can ask forgiveness and you might forgive me. You still, however, have a broken window! You can genuinely forgive me for breaking that window and yet expect me to repair it or pay someone else to do that.

Forgiveness cannot change past facts but it can put them into a new perspective, a more life-giving perspective. For that reason, forgiveness and truth are allies, not enemies. Nothing worthwhile can be built on a lie.

It's much easier to forgive, of course, if the person who should seek forgiveness actually does so. But if that person refuses to admit the harm created by his or her actions, is it foolish for me to forgive?

Some people think their refusal to forgive demonstrates their freedom; in fact, it often shows a *lack* of freedom.

Our experience suggests that bitter, unforgiving people punish themselves more than the people whom they refuse to forgive. The offending people may die without realizing that they should have asked forgiveness. Unforgiving people, however, die with a self-imposed burden that has only grown heavier over time.

Forgiveness is about living in the truth—yes, the truth of my pain, my loss, perhaps someone else's pain or loss—but also the larger truth that the offending person was created in God's image—whether his or her actions reflect that fact. Deep down, forgiveness means wanting for the offending party what God wants for that person: to live honestly as someone made in God's image and likeness, reflecting that in his or her daily choices.

I can forgive a person and still get a restraining order to keep that person away from me. I can forgive someone and still insist that he or she seek professional help to deal with an addiction. I can forgive someone and yet set up a separate bank account. "If you loved me, you would forgive me and not make a big deal out of this," a person might say. You can honestly respond, "It's because I love you that I am making a big deal about this."

It is always appropriate to forgive someone when you can look in the mirror and honestly tell yourself, "I want for that person what God wants." Until you can say that, you should pray for the grace to say it honestly. When you can, then you will be free.

If forgiveness is primarily a gift to oneself, why carry the burden of unforgiveness any longer? Forgiveness can lead to reconciliation but that is not guaranteed. In the Prodigal Son parable, the father had both forgiveness and reconciliation. What if the younger son had never "come to his senses?" Would the father's forgiveness have been wasted? Was the older brother's refusal to forgive a good decision? Perhaps he later forgave his younger brother.

Forgiveness can be one-sided; reconciliation is necessarily two-sided. Forgiveness says: "I am making this step and I hope the other person accepts it—but that other person might die clueless. Even if that happens, forgiving was the right thing to do."

We sometimes balk at forgiveness because what we really want is reconciliation, yet we know that our forgiveness cannot guarantee reconciliation. At times such as these, we need to do the right thing, remembering that God sorts everything out ultimately.

Is Forgiveness Possible?

My wife feels that she needs a miracle to forgive me for the sin of adultery. To her the miracle would be forgiveness and permanently forgetting her mental image of my "dance with the devil," as she describes it.

I have confessed this sin, received absolution, and done that penance. I am truly remorseful, more than words can express. Committed to lifelong reconciliation with her, I have vowed never to commit this sin again.

Can my wife forgive and forget what I have done? She is really struggling with this concept, thinking that if this sin "rears its ugly head" in the future, she will be tempted to follow the devil and sin herself. She is concerned that someday she may weaken as she remembers my sin. She struggles with this human side, wanting to make me suffer consequences for my actions. She feels my reconciliation with God is not enough when she is not being spiritual.

Yes, forgiveness is possible. Despite the popular wisdom, however, that does not require forgetting. Your wife cannot forget what she knows—in this case, your adultery. Even though people blithely speak of "forgive and forget," forgiveness does not require forgetting. Instead it requires that your wife put one fact (your adultery) in the context of many other facts (your love before that incident, your genuine sorrow, and your changed behavior since you admitted this sin).

Your wife can hardly forget your adultery. She may, however, be able to put that in the larger context of a relationship that both of you want to continue and to grow. Both of you may need professional counseling or the help of a program such as Retrouvaille (www.retrouvaille.org or 1-800-470-2230) to do that. This weekend program helps couples deal with various kinds of brokenness in marriage.

The spouse who did not commit adultery certainly cannot prove that adultery is wrong by going out and committing the same sin. Each person needs to accept responsibility for his/her actions, plus their frequently unintended and long-term consequences.

With God's grace, your good will and consistently good decisions by you and your wife, this marriage can survive and be life-giving for both of you as you grow in mutual forgiveness.

Will My Aborted Baby and I Go to Hell?

Three years ago I had an intentional abortion. I was thirteen going on fourteen, not thinking about my baby. I have dreams and I cry every time that anniversary comes around. I am scared that I am going to hell because I did such a terrible thing, and I don't know how to fix it. I am scared my baby will suffer for my choices. Can I save my baby and myself from hell?

Thanks for writing. Your aborted baby has always been in the loving hands of God. There has never been a danger that he or she might go to hell. God's love and mercy have never been withheld from you; I urge you to accept God's forgiveness in the sacrament of reconciliation. If you repent, you certainly will not be condemned.

An intentional abortion is the taking of an innocent human life and is extremely wrong. Many people who think that abortion is a solution for "problem pregnancies" do not want to hear stories such as yours because abortion can create lifelong problems. It is never the solution that some people claim that it is.

In 1984, Project Rachel began as a local ministry to women who have had an abortion; six years later it became a nationwide effort. You can contact Project Rachel (also known as the National Office for Post-abortion Reconciliation and Healing) at www.noparh.org or at 1-800-5WE-CARE in complete confidentiality.

Project Rachel now works with parents and grandparents of women who have had abortions and with men whose wives or girlfriends did likewise. Friends, siblings, and other relatives are also affected by a decision to abort. Project Rachel can help in many ways.

You realize that what you did was very wrong. What you may not realize is that no sin is beyond God's power to forgive. If it were, the sin would be greater than God—and that is not possible.

Project Rachel, which is active in almost every diocese in the United States, can direct you to a specially trained confessor in your area. Or you could set up an appointment for confession with a Catholic priest in your area. Yours will not be the first such confession he has heard, and he is there to represent God's forgiveness. May the Lord always be your strength and guide.

Can the Sin of Abortion Be Forgiven?

I have read that abortion results in excommunication from the Catholic Church. Does this apply to the woman who had it, those who may have pressured her into that decision, and those who work in abortion clinics? Is it possible to receive absolution for this sin?

People who are truly sorry can be absolved from their direct or indirect involvement in the sin of abortion. In our January 1988 issue, Father Norman Perry, O.F.M., wrote:

> Canon 1398 of the present Code of Canon Law says, "A person who actually procures an abortion incurs a *latae sententiae* excommunication."

"That means a Catholic woman who has an abortion—and accomplices without whose assistance the offense would not have been committed (Canon 1329, #2)—is excommunicated automatically by the law itself if all the other requirements of the code are present.

"Those conditions are as follows: 1) The abortion was directly intended and was successful. It was not a case of miscarriage or accidental loss of the child; 2) The woman involved knew the penalty was attached to the law forbidding abortion; 3) She was at least 18 years old at the time of the abortion; 4) She had the full use of reason (she did not have Down syndrome or was not psychologically disturbed); 5) She did not act out of serious fear.

"If the woman (or accomplice, e.g., the abortionist) has incurred the penalty of excommunication, canon law (Canon 1355, #2) gives the local ordinary (the bishop) power to remit it. Many bishops delegate all confessors to absolve from this excommunication without recourse to themselves—at least in the case of a first abortion."

This means that in most United States dioceses any priest who has the faculties of the diocese can absolve from this sin and excommunication the first time.

Pope John Paul II's 1995 encyclical *Evangelium Vitae*, Gospel of Life, includes this passage: "I would like to say a special word to women who have had an abortion. The Church is aware of the many factors which may have influences your decision, and she does not doubt that in many cases it was a painful and even shattering decision. The wound in your heart may not yet have healed. Certainly what happened was and remains terribly wrong. But do not give in to discouragement and do not lose hope. Try rather to understand what happened and face it honestly.

"If you have not already done so, give yourselves over with humility and trust to repentance. The Father of mercies is ready to give you his forgiveness and his peace in the Sacrament of Reconciliation. You will come to understand that nothing is definitely lost and you will also be able to ask forgiveness from your child, who is now living in the Lord" (#99).

For over twenty-five years, Project Rachel (see previous Q&A) has ministered to women who have had abortions, families that have been touched by abortions, and people who have facilitated someone else's abortion. Project Rachel, which is listed in the Resource section of this book, also offers special training for confessors of people who seek to be absolved of this sin.

Can Only Catholics Be Saved?

Do Catholics believe that the only way to Christ and to salvation is through the Catholic faith? Can non-Catholics be saved? Are Catholics guaranteed salvation?

The term "non-Catholics" includes other Christians who are baptized as well as people who have never been baptized. Yes, people from both groups can be saved.

Section 1260 of the *Catechism of the Catholic Church* begins by saying, "Since Christ died for all, and since all men are in fact called to one and the same destiny, which is divine, we must hold that the Holy Spirit offers to all the possibility of being made partakers, in a way known to God, of the Paschal mystery." Those words are quoted from Vatican II's *Lumen Gentium,* Pastoral Constitution on the Church in the Modern World, (#22); the Catechism links them to the same council's Dogmatic Constitution on the Church (#16) and its Decree on the Church's Missionary Activity (#7).

Section 1260 of the *Catechism* continues: "Every man who is ignorant of the Gospel of Christ and of his Church, but seeks the truth and does the will of God in accordance with his understanding of it, can be saved. It may be supposed that such persons would have *desired Baptism explicitly* if they had known of its necessity."

Some people interpret such statements as undermining the urgency of preaching the good news of Jesus, as he commanded in Matthew 28:19 ("Go therefore and make disciples of all nations, baptizing them in the name of the Father and of the Son and of the holy Spirit") and related passages. Such an interpretation is mistaken.

Those who are baptized must share the good news with others, especially through the testimony of a life that reflects that good news and the person's baptism. No one can explicitly know Jesus Christ today without the help of the faith community that he established. That faith community had a single name for one thousand years (Catholic or Christian) and then split into two groups (Eastern Orthodox and

Roman Catholic) in the eleventh century. Some Eastern Catholic Churches existed before that split and others arose after it. In the sixteenth century and afterward, Western Christianity split into more groups.

No one today can leapfrog over history into direct contact with Jesus Christ in the same way that the twelve apostles knew him. We consider the Bible to be the Word of God because the faith community, to which it was given, tells us that it is.

Not all Catholics or other Christians have cooperated with the grace of their baptism. That sacrament initiates a person into a new relationship with God but does not put God "over a barrel" (so to speak) regarding that person's salvation. Sins can be forgiven but they must be acknowledged first. A murderer or a rapist, for example, could defy God to the very end of that person's life.

God alone knows each person's heart and how each one has responded to God's grace—whether that person was baptized or not.

Do Catholics and Lutherans Now Agree on Faith and Good Works?

I heard that in October 1999 the pope signed a document to unite all Christians. Could you please explain what that means? Was there a compromise regarding Catholic traditions and beliefs? Where can I find more information about this document?

I think you are referring to an historic agreement between Roman Catholics and Lutherans—not a document to unite *all* Christians. A "Joint Declaration on Justification" was indeed signed in Augsburg, Germany on October 31, 1999, on behalf of the Roman Catholic Church and the Lutheran World Federation.

That document reflects thirty years of ecumenical dialogue between these two churches and effectively ends a four-hundred-year-old doctrinal dispute. The Holy See's Pontifical Council for Promoting Christian Unity helped develop this Joint Declaration, which had been approved by the Holy See's Congregation for the Doctrine of the Faith and by Pope John Paul II, who sent representatives to sign the Declaration on behalf of the Catholic Church.

Justification is the teaching about how people are saved. This teaching was probably the most basic difference between Roman Catholics and Martin Luther in the sixteenth century.

The Joint Declaration says: "The understanding of the doctrine of justification set forth in this declaration shows that a consensus in basic truths exists between Lutherans and Catholics [#40]...The teaching of the Lutheran churches presented in this declaration does not fall under the condemnations from the Council of Trent. The condemnations in the Lutheran Confessions do not apply to the teaching of the Roman Catholic Church presented in this declaration [#41]."

The Lutheran World Federation then represented fifty-eight million of the world's sixty-one million Lutherans; this document was approved according to official procedures of that federation and the Holy See.

When the Joint Declaration was initially approved in June 1998, both sides identified issues needing resolution before the declaration could be accepted as an official statement from these Christians. A further "Common Statement" and "Annex" were released by both sides on June 11, 1999; they are part of the document that was signed in Augsburg, Germany, where the foundational Lutheran *Augsburg Confession* on justification was drawn up in 1530.

The following are two key passages: "Together we confess: By grace alone, in faith in Christ's saving work and not because of any merit on our part, we are accepted by God and receive the Holy Spirit, who renews our hearts while equipping can calling us to good words" (#15); and "Grace, as fellowship of the justified with God in faith, hope and love, is always received from the salvific and creative work of God. But it is nevertheless the responsibility of the justified not to waste this grace but to live in it. The exhortation to do good works is the exhortation to practice the faith" ("Annex," #2D).

You can be sure that the Congregation for the Doctrine of the Faith very carefully carried out its responsibilities and would not have approved this new document if it had compromised the Catholic faith.

You can find the text of the Joint Declaration at www.zenit.org/ English. Since many Protestants other than Lutherans consider the *Augsburg Confession* a foundational document, they have taken notice of this Joint Declaration.

Is Judas in Hell?

In Matthew 26:24, Jesus says, "The Son of Man goes as it is written of him, but woe to that one by whom the Son of Man is betrayed! It would have been better for that one not to have been born."

In John 13:27 we read, "After he [Judas Iscariot] received the piece of bread, Satan entered him. Jesus said to him, 'Do quickly what you are going to do.'" From preachers and others, I have heard different views as to whether Judas is definitely in hell or perhaps was forgiven. Is there biblical justification for one view or the other?

In some ways, this might seem the easiest judgment of all to make. Judas betrayed Jesus, our savior, leading to his passion, death, and resurrection. Judas obviously made a terrible decision.

Although we need to be clear about the objective content of any decision (for example, the unlawful taking of innocent human life is murder), it is another thing to say that we know all the factors relevant to that decision and can, therefore, pass God's judgment as accurately as God can. That is a form of idolatry, in effect shoving God out of the way as though we fear that God cannot be trusted to make the right decision.

God's judgment must always remain God's judgment. We try to grow toward seeing things as God sees them, but if we cannot be sure that we see our own actions as completely as God does (and we cannot be 100-percent sure of that), then we cannot be absolutely certain that we see someone else's actions as clearly and accurately as God sees them.

Shouldn't it tell us something that after careful examination the Catholic Church is quite willing to say that a certain individual is definitely in heaven yet refuses to say that someone else is certainly in hell? I am not aware that any Christian group has drawn up a formal list of individuals who are certainly in hell. Dante's *Inferno* makes for interesting reading, but it does not necessarily reflect God's judgment. Anyone's list could be mistaken.

Although it is quite clear that some actions are very sinful, being a "grave matter" is one of *three* conditions for identifying a mortal sin. The other two are "full knowledge" and "full consent." Only God can judge with absolute certainty the presence or absence of those two conditions.

Two things must be kept in mind: If I deny that eternal separation from God is a possibility, I am guilty of heresy. If I claim to know absolutely that a particular individual is in hell, I am guilty of blasphemy, of claiming as mine a knowledge that belongs to God alone. Human judgments do not give God a day off!

There is ample biblical justification for saying that what Judas did was gravely wrong. The same Bible, however, cautions us to leave God's judgment of individuals to God.

For the good of society, we must make prudential judgments about how to handle people who murder, individuals who steal, and so on. But those are human judgments and should not be assumed to reflect God's definitive judgments.

The *Catechism of the Catholic Church* reminds us that the church prays that no person be lost. It also reminds us "that God 'desires all men to be saved' (1 *Tim* 2:4), and that for him 'all things are possible' (Mt 19:26)" (#1058).

The story of Judas' betrayal of Jesus is important for Christians to know, but they can keep growing as disciples without knowing if Judas is, in fact, in hell. We can hope that he repented even if we are not sure that he did.

What Does the Church Say About Limbo?

The teaching about limbo has me perplexed because it casts into doubt whether babies who die before being baptized can be saved. Are they sent to limbo? Are aborted babies doubly punished?

About forty years ago, a missionary conducted a novena at our parish and preached that God is a loving and forgiving God. The priest urged us to ask God to love and forgive us. Why then should so many souls be sent to limbo?

On April 20, 2007, the thirty-member International Theological Commission (ITC) published, with Pope Benedict XVI's permission, a forty-one-page document entitled *The Hope of Salvation for Infants Who Die Without Being Baptized*. This is the result of a study begun in 2004 by the ITC, whose members are appointed by the pope and work with the Congregation for the Doctrine of the Faith (CDF). This ITC document is available at the CDF section of www.vatican.va.

This document says that the traditional concept of limbo as a place where unbaptized infants spend eternity but without communion with God seems to reflect "an unduly restrictive view of salvation."

"Our conclusion is that the many factors that we have considered…give serious theological and liturgical grounds for hope that unbaptized infants who die will be saved and enjoy the beatific vision." The text added, "We emphasize that these are reasons for prayerful hope, rather than grounds for sure knowledge."

This ITC document is not as authoritative a teaching as a papal document, but the *Catechism of the Catholic Church* never mentions limbo. It teaches "As regards *children who have died without Baptism*, the Church can only entrust them to the mercy of God, as she does in her funeral rites for them" (#1261).

Cardinal Joseph Ratzinger (now Pope Benedict XVI) stated in 1984 when he was prefect of the CDF: "Limbo was never a defined truth of faith. Personally—and here I am speaking more as a theologian and not as prefect of the Congregation—I would abandon it since it was only a theological hypothesis. It formed part of a secondary thesis in support of a truth which is absolutely of first significance for faith, namely, the importance of Baptism" (*The Ratzinger Report*, p. 147).

In the eleventh century, Saint Anselm of Canterbury described theology as "faith seeking understanding." The ITC's document described above is an example of such faith.

Many Catholics long ago came to the same conclusion about limbo as the ITC. Apparently the mission preacher whom you remember did. Over the years, Father Norman Perry, O.F.M., the previous author of the "Ask" column, and I have reflected this in replies to this question.

Some people have thought that limbo was necessary for unbaptized infants because of Jesus' teaching, "Very truly, I tell you, no one can see the kingdom of God without being born from above" (John 3:3).

The concept of limbo arose in regard to children who die without being baptized, but the same reasoning was applied to adults who lived after Jesus but who died without baptism. Accordingly, the best that the majority of adults who have ever lived could hope for was limbo.

In section four of the Declaration on the Relation of the Church to Non-Christian Religions, the bishops at Vatican II taught, "Together with the prophets and that same apostle [Paul], the Church awaits the day, known to God alone, when all peoples will call on God with one voice and 'serve him shoulder to shoulder' (Zephaniah 3:9; see also Isaiah 66:23; Psalm 65:4 and Romans 11:11–32)."

The sacrament of baptism remains very important, but having received it does not guarantee that someone will be saved. Likewise, not having received it does not mean that a person cannot be saved. That is up to God alone.

What Does the Church Teach About Reincarnation?

One of my close friends believes in reincarnation. My Catholic education and faith leave me with no reason to believe in multiple lives. My friend claims that all mention of reincarnation was removed from the Bible in the early centuries of the church.

Please provide me with some background on reincarnation, its presence in the Bible at any time in history and the Catholic Church's position on it.

In *A Concise Dictionary of Theology* (Paulist), Jesuits Gerald O'Collins and Edward Farugia describe reincarnation as "the belief, also called *metempsychosis* (Greek for 'animate afterwards'), that souls inhabit a series of bodies and can live many lives on this earth before being completely purified and so released from the need to migrate to another body.

"According to this belief, the soul preexists its embodiment, and after death exists in a disembodied state before animating [inhabiting] once again a body of the same or a different species. In various forms, reincarnation has been accepted by Buddhists, Hindus, Neo-Platonists, and others.

"Belief in resurrection and official rejection of the preexistence of souls...rule out reincarnation. By maintaining an indefinite series of chances, the doctrine of reincarnation reduces the seriousness of God's grace and human liberty exercise in one life that is terminated by a once-and-for-all death."

In 1991 the Holy See's International Theological Commission published *Certain Aspects of Eschatology*, which says: "Christianity defends *duality*; reincarnation defends a *dualism* in which the body is simply an instrument of the soul and is laid aside, existence by successive existence, as an altogether different body is assumed each time.

"As far as eschatology is concerned, the doctrine of reincarnation denies both the possibility of eternal damnation and the idea of the resurrection of the body. But the fundamental error is in the rejection of the Christian doctrine of salvation. For the reincarnationist the soul is its own savior by its own efforts" (Section 9.3).

Reincarnation denies the need to convert, about which Jesus spoke often. If souls keep recycling, won't they all end up in the same place eventually? If so, why are any of our decisions today important?

There is absolutely no evidence that reincarnation was originally in the Bible but was later removed. Conspiracy theorists love to assert that later church authorities have removed things from the Bible. That is simply not true.

The *Catechism of the Catholic Church* says: "When 'the single course of our earthly life' is completed, we shall not return to other earthly lives: 'It is appointed for men to die once' [Hebrews 9:27]. There is no 'reincarnation' after death" (#1013).

Resources

The Web sites and 800-numbers presented in the text are listed here for your convenience.

Holy See (www.vatican.va). Documents from congregations or pontifical councils can be accessed through that office's link at www.vatican.va/roman_curia/index.htm.

National Catholic Bioethics Center (www.ncbcenter.org).

Project Rachel (also known as the National Office for Post-abortion Reconciliation and Healing), www.noparh.org or 1-800-5WE-CARE.

Retrouvaille (www.retrouvaille.org or 1-800-470-2230).

St. Anthony Messenger Press (www.AmericanCatholic.org). This links to the archived magazine articles, editorials, or columns cited in the text. Through the Parish Resources link, back issues of *Catholic Update* newsletters cited in this book can be read.

United States Conference of Catholic Bishops (www.usccb.org).

ABOUT THE AUTHOR

FR. PAT MCCLOSKEY, O.F.M., is the editor of *St. Anthony Messenger* magazine and author of its "Ask a Franciscan" column. He holds master's degrees in theology, divinity, and Franciscan studies. Author of six books and many articles, he has also revised and updated St. Anthony Messenger Press's bestselling titles *Believing in Jesus* and *Saint of the Day*.